Ms Roberta N Damberg
755 White Elm Dr
Loveland CO 80538-2807

The Tale of Three Cities

Gran Quivira, New Mexico
1906

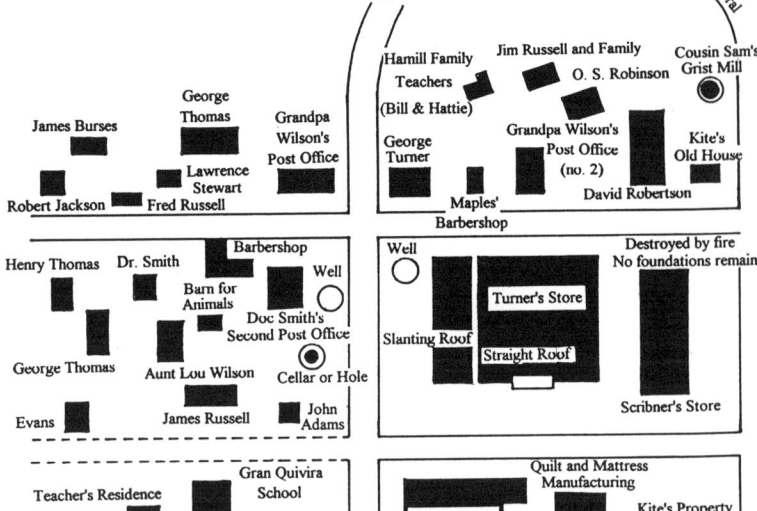

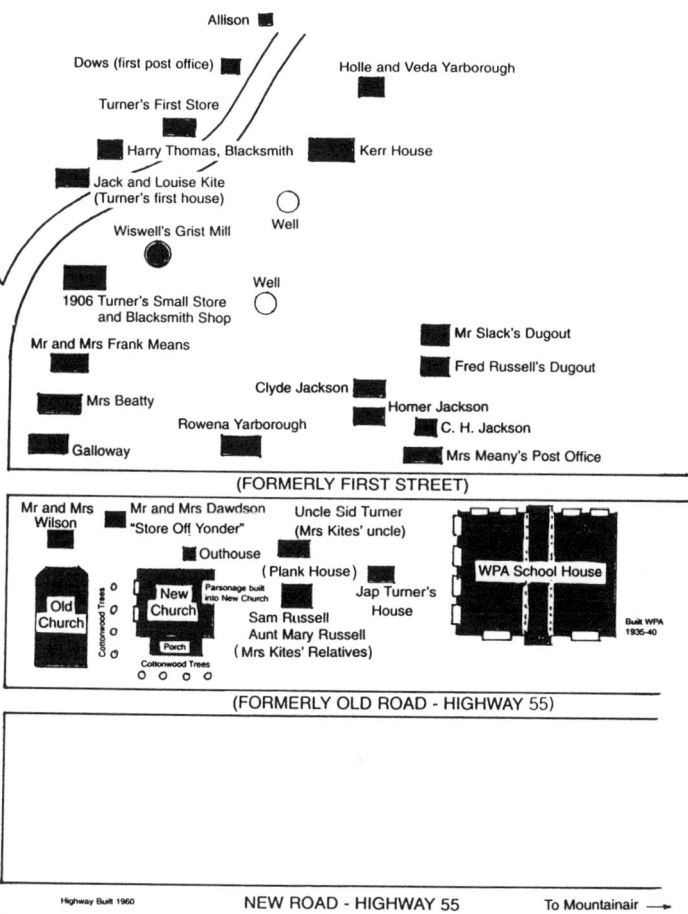

The Tale of Three Cities

Gran Quivira in the Southwest
New Mexico, 1100 B.C. to A.D. 1963

Eugene P. Link and
Beulah M. Link

With a Contribution by Gordon L. McMath

VANTAGE PRESS
New York

Poems of Freda Walker Brown used by permission of Gordon L. McMath. All portraits used by the gracious permission of Ernest D. Garcia, representative of the Dow-Garcia families. Map of Gran Quivira, New Mexico (1997), courtesy of Harry R. Forrest.

FIRST EDITION

All rights reserved, including the right of
reproduction in whole or in part in any form.

Copyright © 1999 by Eugene P. Link and Beulah M. Link

Published by Vantage Press, Inc.
516 West 34th Street, New York, New York 10001

Manufactured in the United States of America
ISBN: 0-533-12461-1

Library of Congress Catalog Card No.: 97-90704

0 9 8 7 6 5 4 3 2 1

To all human beings who have lived on the land that is now Torrance County, New Mexico, from the years 0 to A.D. 2000, for their role in human history

Contents

Introduction: The View, the Vista, and the Viewpoint of
    Gran Quivira I, II, III   xi

1. "Alas, Poor Yorick": Gran Quivira I   1
2. Emerging from the Earth, Reaching for the Heavens:
    The Second City Appears, Fifteenth Century   6
3. The Third Gran Quivira Emerges: End of the
    Nineteenth Century   13
4. Politics, Peanuts, Piety   28
5. The Valley Is Still There, By Gordon L. McMath,
    Citizen of the Third City   38
6. The Book of Days: Vital Records from Gran Quivira   60

Our Last Words   95

Appendixes
Appendix A: Interview with Jack and Louise Kite,
    January 21, 1996   101
Appendix B: Residents of Gran Quivira   105
Appendix C: Teachers in Gran Quivira Schools as Recalled
    by Louise Kite   107
Appendix D: Selected Readings   109

Introduction: The View, the Vista, and the Viewpoint of Gran Quivira I, II, III

This book is a vista rather than a limited view bounded by dates and discreteness. Charles Beard, a towering historian of the departed century, stated that people involved only with serial or episodic views become dizzy, discouraged, artless, and naive. They fall off the train of history as it twists and makes U-turns at breathtaking speeds into the future. A vista is a steadier view, making for a more sound interpretation of the past and the present.

In the very center of enchanting New Mexico is an area called the Salinas Valley. An observer can find any number of vistas that belonged here centuries before Columbus dropped anchor somewhere in the Caribbean. A portion of this Salinas Valley has been labeled Gran Quivira. This *first* Gran Quivira is the area where prehistory humans lived, moved and had their being in "cities" dating roughly from A.D. 500 to A.D. 1100 and constructed in a pit house groupings. These primitive groups were abandoned. The *second* general area was first labeled unspecifically as Gran Quivira by the dreamer-adventurer Coronado. He was certain many golden cities called *cibolos* were about to be found. Approximately one-half mile east from the first Gran Quivira pit houses stands a rock-walled derelict city. It is partially excavated and is constructed of white limestone into a "Spanish Cathedral" reminding us of the cathedracentric towns of Europe. This Gran Quivira included Humanos and Anasazi Indians who lived in pueblos and were absorbed into the Spanish Entrada. It was abandoned in 1672.

Almost equidistant between the umbilical-like pit houses and Gran Quivira II on the hill is Gran Quivira III. This touch of urbanity is established in United States records as a post office. Abandoned a little after the middle of this century, the village today resembles a ghost town. It is marked by several derelict rock huts and stores and peeping foundations where at one time 800 citizens worked and lived.

This book is an appreciation of our opportunity to become affiliated with the National Park Service as VIPs—"Volunteers In Parks." From 1987 to 1991, we spent four consecutive winters working four eight-hour days per week. We chose, along with other daily tasks, to research a segment of the Salinas National Pueblo Park's glorious history, namely the hamlet of Gran Quivira whose dates are roughly from 1875 to 1965. The United States Post Office existed from 1904 to 1963.

We doubt the tale of this little city in sparsely settled New Mexico could be rivaled by any other— at least not one that within a ninety-year span revealed such speed in clearly demarcated change. It was affected by two turnovers in population—from American Indians to Spanish to Anglo—and three major types of agriculture have surrounded it: subsistence farming and sheep raising, cattle raising and feeding, and bean farming.

Gran Quivira became inflated by growing pinto beans for the doughboys in World War I. The nearest urban-like area was Mountainair, a railroad water stop that was labeled, along with Gran Quivira at times, the "Bean Capitol of the World."

The first settler of Gran Quivira III was Elisha Dow, the son of a college president from Iowa. He married a Spanish princess and sired a large and useful family. The maligned folk hero Billy the Kid roamed the streets freely and created neither fear nor violence. An extraordinary blind woman, Clara Corbin, of Victorian speech and dress and a published writer, lived in the ruins of the "Spanish Cathedral" for twenty years. Some of the now ubiquitous and mammoth Assembly of God congregations held several state conventions in the history of Gran Quivira III.

During the era of this study, the Gran Quivira area was virtually an Anglo island in a sea of Latino and indigenous Americans. The latter left Gran Quivira and Spanish settlers like Elisha Dow and others had moved northward to the Santa Fe area. The Anglo population came as a result of homestead possibilities and the healthful climate for which New Mexico was becoming popular. The insularity of the village made it a vehicle to introduce and maintain the "American" character.

We wish to thank those who represent the National Park Service and oversee the Salinas Monuments, of which Gran Quivira is one, for their generous help and encouragement. Rudy Baca, the former superintendent, and Glenn Fulfer, the new one, were constantly alert with sound suggestions for us. One in particular was the exciting chore of aiding them in preserving the people's parks from the continuous search for sneaking gold thieves, as well as maintaining the shimmering white stones from further disarray by energetic climbers. Superintendent Baca's predecessor, Tom Carroll, and Melody Webb from the central office in Santa Fe did much to induce us to come to the Gran Quivira Park before we signed a contract. Park Rangers Carol Chilton and Ernestine Cisnaros gave generously of their time, energy, and knowledge, and guided us to books, pamphlets, old photographs, and other sources. Sylvia Lewis, the National Park secretary, and her mother brought us personal anecdotes of those buried in the town cemetery. Sam Chavez, whose family origins were among the Tonorios, who arrived as settlers almost as soon as Dow did, helped us with the story of the Spanish arrivals.

There are many people beyond the borders of the park who assisted us to, we hope, compile a more humanistic story about this intriguing place. First to mind are Jack and Louise Kite, sturdy New Mexican farmers and ranchers whose skin is parched by the weather, whose eyes are faded to pale blue even though they both have had permanent squints to protect them. Both are rugged in a beautiful way as wind, rain, sun, and sand have chiseled and furrowed special designs into their faces, and rugged also in a way that makes them people of stature, in body and mind. Louise offered us cookies, the kind you seldom get—flavored by burning mesquite! In their eighties, they watch after one another and their roles are, generally and as need demands, interchangeable. Louise Kite, with the greatest devotion, walked the parameters of Gran Quivira with Beulah Link so many times, identifying places where homes, schools, churches, a mattress factory, and general stores had been located, to preserve the history of this unusual place, now a ghost town.

During the four years we were volunteers, much of our free time was given to interviewing and recording many of the citizens (perhaps almost all) who had lived in Gran Quivira III before 1965. We interviewed Spanish-speaking families beginning with descendants of Elisha Dow, the Garcias, the Tonarios, and others who were marginally or often directly involved. Their stories, some in typescript and others on tape, have been given to the Coronado Room, University of New Mexico, for historical research and safekeeping.

To visit and work in an area where such dramatic changes have taken place in the lives of average people in the last thousand years is exciting. This historical process has involved Native, Black, Spanish, and Anglo peoples. It is also timely because it lends examples of ongoing cultural interaction and clash, which need informed attention as we press on to build our "global city." It can furnish a microcosmic study which might be valuable in the future to approach vistas for United States history and our National Parks.

All the people in and around Gran Quivira, without exception, went the second mile for us. They helped our recorder to function properly, repeated conversations for accuracy, brought us refreshments, and sent us away with joy brimming over in a way that only William Allen White of Kansas or William J. Bryan of Nebraska (our home states) could have adequately put into words. This is in many ways a "peoples" book.

The Tale of Three Cities

1
"Alas, Poor Yorick": Gran Quivira I

What can be written about the first Gran Quivira? Only a little, in truth, because solid evidence is confined to stones, bones shaped and scratched by humans seeking to express themselves, to tell their story without leaving a translation. The whitened skull uncovered by the grave digger doesn't speak when addressed by the young Prince Hamlet, "Alas, Poor Yorick, what secrets you could divulge."

Jugs, vases, and tools that are unquestionable artifacts but also the rocklike bones dug up by careful hands are solid evidence. Alas, poor femur, you bore much food and water to satiate others; and alas, poor lassie-bones spread in childbirth to ensure the continuity of life. Hence one can be certain of the existence of social bonds among the pit dwellers in the area later to be named Gran Quivira. These early people running back into limbo assist in the quest for the vista outlook of history, making it a better guide for thought and understanding than gathering facts, somewhat meaninglessly set, as they usually are, in small time frames. Quite by accident, the pit dwellers helped in the appreciation of the two other Gran Quiviras to come.

By the use of the probing tools of *assumption, surmise, projection,* and *inference*—all indicating a kind of special quality of human mind—it is possible to look into the skull's deep hollow eyes and say, "you must have been able to . . ." or "we might infer" that because of "this" there must have been "that." Probability is more valid if supported by a measure of logic.

The modern anthropologist and archeologist would be greatly hampered if deprived of the right to the intelligent guess. In fact, it has grown more sophisticated aided by sociology, chemistry, geology, physics, and biology. The pit people reveal to us that they were social animals who slowly seemed to give up rugged individualism by forming social groups for defense, for hunting, for providing water, and for better houses.

At the dawn of history, human beings undoubtedly lived in caves, in cists, and behind rocks. The earliest Quivirians seemed to have lived in pits. In back of Jack and Louise Kite's home, archeologists dug into an eroded stream bed to discover what doubtless were hide-covered pit houses. Could it have been a "sanctuary" similar to those of the ancient Eskimo, where no one could be struck a blow if within the home circle? Outside the circle one could maul another pit man or woman with death-dealing blows.

These pit houses of Gran Quivira were explored by Alison Rautman, a skilled archeologist armed with an abundance of refined, scientific aids. She reasoned that they lived in groups, united by social and ethical codes necessary for survival. A small pit was occasionally identified, but a large agglomeration was clearly apparent, always near a water supply.

These clusters of life seemed to have clung to the rugged banks of a stream that at one time brought water from the Chupadera Mountains down to them. In a small way, the story anticipated the ubiquitous river valley civilizations of the Zambesi, the Nile, the Indus, the Yellow—all washed-out relics to titillate the imagination of scholars. Gran Quivira I, in the Kite's backyard, is only one example in the sweep of history that after a flooding exposed remnants of humans' acting, interacting, and reacting.

Of course, life on the banks of the arroyo grew more and more complex as the years passed. The villagers learned to utilize corn as a good food to grind, cook, eat, and use as a substance in religious ceremonies. It became "the bread of life" to be eaten as the body of their Earth Mother in silence and devotion. Corn and later other grains were hand-ground, not in a grist mill but in a special place—the "mealing room"—operated by the women of the family. There is sufficient evidence that men did the weaving and much of the growing of squash and later beans.

By A.D. 700, grey clay pots and vessels were found, decorated with varying black stripes and designs. From approximately A.D. 799, the pit people have been identified as "Basketmakers," the baskets woven so tightly they could hold water. On a visit to the Kite village area, one could view many pieces of this ancient pottery. Researchers have succeeded in matching the shards, as they are called. The result has been the exposure of centuries of human creativity.

In areas to the southwest and to the north of this prehistoric Gran Quivira village were, respectively, the Mogollon and Tampiro people, the latter making reddish-tinged pots with black stripes. Rautman's use of the "environmental context" to make inferences about the finding of a tiny shard of red with black stripes among the gray and black reveals that visitors and traders came to Gran Quivira I. The more carefully studied and preserved the most minuscule detritus in the environmental context, the more is learned of how people coped (the word Rautman uses) with one another and the physical world.

Charles A. Beard and Mary R. Beard were enjoying tea after several hours of writing when Mary asked, "Charles, in the seventies, life is getting precarious. If I survive you, what should be carved on your gravestone?" After a pause, he answered, "Here lies Charles Beard, who spent his life discovering a few obvious things." This obviousness is in the astute studies of Patricia Gilman and Kent Lightfoot, archeologists who, like Rautman, are searching to know more about the pit dwellers. Look at the obvious things, the pit houses, jacals and kivas. They are striking proxemic artifacts. The structures tell about the seasons by the flora around them; the heat-cold and the wet-dry cycles; or the population pressures for seasonal protection; or how far below ground and how thick were the low walls—variations such as thickness on one or another side. Environment prompts various architectural forms.

Lightfoot's hypotheses can cast some light on leadership patterns in this the most ancient Gran Quivira. Obviously, leaders are socially magnetic. They bring other humans into the situation. If an ancient room is congested with artifacts, it may belong to a leader; or if more food is stored there, it underlines the traditional lifestyle in most history of overfeeding the king and the priest. The accumulation of pit homes could mean someone of importance was in their midst, especially if the surrounding pits were smaller and some were found in a similar outlay at Kite's Gran Quivira. Again, we might infer that more agricultural activity would surround the pits of the "banker" and the "senator." The insightfully trained archeologist knows who gets most and eats most. Extra supplies of things are brought to his door for trading and close by ("yes," says Professor Lightfoot) the researchers find a plethora of flint flakes lying around where instruments of aggression were made to protect the leader's opulence from all scrawny thieving hands. Gran Quivira I's surroundings can give us a partial picture of its people and their activities, but not a full one. For example, the youth received sex education, but it was hardly formalized. Mothers showed daughters how to staunch the monthly flow with the dried silk from their revered corn. Their "informal" education was real and necessary. Everyone walked for miles, often carrying heavy loads of water and other necessities. One can understand this but they also seemed to keep moving to new locations. Practical needs, especially water, could be a frequent reason. Recent scholars have reverted to genetics for answers, claiming a peripatetic gene appeared dominant. Better guesses seem to be the 500-year weather cycles. Each time people moved, the pit dwellings were abandoned. It must have been difficult to leave their circular homes, now rapidly becoming sanctuaries where Mother Earth arose at times, just to advise and consent. No wonder the Native Americans left their collectively owned land, preserved the flora and fauna, and started—in about A.D. 900 to 1000—to erect larger cities rising from the earth, which are usually identified as towns or pueblos.

The first Gran Quivira grew into a more unified village in what would become Rancher Kite's backyard. These folk, including those within the boundaries of the park, for a moment in history seemed to have united food, clothing, and shelter with family life, government, religion, and art, so closely that the stealthy anthropologist has trouble naming which kind of "coping" is going on in any social situation.

In the next moment in history, give or take several centuries, this earliest Gran Quivira had disappeared, covered over by the force of winds, floods, and blowing sand filling crevices. The village and its trickle water flow are apparent only after rare and brief floodtides sweep through the arroyo. Then the eye of the questioner, alert with a spade, a whisk, and a feather brush, has been able to perpetuate history, writing of more of its gifts for living better. By pondering the vista, we project more safely.

2

Emerging from the Earth, Reaching for the Heavens: The Second City Appears, Fifteenth Century

The eleventh to the thirteenth centuries in the valley found popping up, like peyote buttons from the soil, jacals, pit houses, and kivas. These were encircled by rocks turned upward to the sky to assist the formation of a ring of poles. Hides were thrown across the perpendicular stakes to protect the inhabitants from the weather. One wonders—was this the beginning of a skyscraper impulse, so characteristic in human dwellings for centuries, or was it a gene that made "upness" a force not to be denied?

Other transitions have moved inexorably toward safer and more permanent living quarters. One was "let's get closer together by using masonry and hitching our discreet jacals together to form 'I' or 'L' designs." The leaning technique tended to displace rows of unsteady stakes and was a step upward in social evolution as well as an unconscious forming of more aesthetic patterns of layout. By 1425, sandstone and limestone pueblos four and five stories "up" were reaching for the stars from the Gila Canyons area to Mesa Verde and beyond. They leaned on rock cliffs.

As the Anasazi Indians moved through the mountains and into the eastern uplands, their structures were at ground level on high places. Rocks they could barely carry were now chosen for giving the stability that was lost by leaving canyon cliffs. Both the careful studies of archeologists John Ivey and Alison Trautman underline the theme of how a village (or a city) is molded by its cultural ecology Equally, as Winston Churchill wrote, "We build our buildings and our buildings build our lives." We stand taller and see farther.

While this interaction was moving toward the formation of the fabulous, imposing walls of Gran Quivira II of the seventeenth century, some dark clouds on the horizon warned of culture clash between the native people and other men with gleaming sails on their ships, who rode astride snorting white beasts that breathed fire. The Native Americans were as doomed as the Aegean Greek states were when they faced the Hyksos on their fast mounts. If history tends to repeat itself then the Gallic invaders who sacked Rome were barbarians too, and the Spaniards who smashed the Aztec and the Incas' buildings as well. The Anasazi were equally blameworthy and destructive if blaming is able to solve the permeating cruelties and ruthless action of history. Human beings have used the most horrible means at hand to destroy and enslave.

In the vista view of history, shocking and painful as it often is, social heterosis turns the earthy constructions of the lowly pit houses into a Gran Quivira built of rock and resting securely on it. Archeologists from many universities and museums have given careful study to Gran Quivira II. They and the feverish gold seekers who dug deep shafts near the sturdy walls in search of riches have collectively brought a wealth of information. The modern scholars have, by their careful excavations, uncovered the largest visible pueblo in the Rio Grande Valley. Although much more is available to be studied and mused over—as Hamlet used Yorick's skull—also much more has been written about the artifacts, and given considerable knowledge of the now extinct Native American group called Las Humanas. No writing has been found, leaving Gran Quivira's first five hundred years shrouded in the mysteries surrounding their pit house forebears. What we do have on record need not be copied here, but it must be used to expand the vista view of history as the centuries swept from pit house to pueblo.

Dwellings, then, hugging the cramped pit house, pushed upward to become cliff dwellings for more sedentary living, for the storage of food and for living space, to accommodate an ever-growing population. As groups grow larger they tend to segmentize sometimes by lineage or by function, giving rise to the need for more rooms for each additional new segment created. Space becomes more specialized so that masonry is needed not solely for protection, but also to hide matters of secrecy like sex behavior, rites of passage, and other religious formalities.

From basketmakers, Gran Quivirans turned more and more to become masons and then ceramicists. Their buildings at places rose to three or four stories as their baskets and pottery became more sophisticated. Roofs were made of small cross-lain sticks, twigs, or reeds. These, of course, have not survived the weathering of the centuries.

Fire was moved to the outside for the cooking of healthful vegetables like cholla pod, prickly pear cactus, yucca flowers flavored with seeds, roots, and pinyon nuts. These Quivirans raised corn, squash, and beans and had learned to chip out arrows large enough to overcome a pronghorn and sufficiently small to down rabbits and quail.

Before the *entrada* of the Spanish, there is evidence that the Humanas people traded bison hides and meat for corn with their neighbors, the Apache. After the invasion of the Spanish, economic exploitation and competition led to raids and killings between the Pueblo and the Apache of the plains. This process so weakened the Indians they were able to be enslaved more easily by the Spanish.

Every possible invention was contrived to gather and preserve water, especially when the Rio Grande confronted a dry cycle, which seemed to occur at intervals of seven to ten generations.

In between these, the land was fertile and bountiful for a century or more. The story of the three Quivira settlements is awesomely twisted and turned into opposites by these cycles of life and death. The white-grey sandstone pueblo city set high on the mesa gleams in the morning sun but it becomes a deadly desert when all efforts fail to preserve water. The Pueblo people were ingenious in digging wells in sandy valleys, in damming streams in arroyos when rain came, in the use of cisterns, and in the necessity of using their urine in place of water to make tight masonry in the later days of one of those droughts.

Activities both to contain and to distribute water in order to erect multiple-storied rooms with masonry suggest the need for a centralized government of some sophistication. By inference, we may believe the village had leaders, councils, and other representative bodies—otherwise how would it be determined who was eligible to live in the "apartment house"? This very process sparked formations of family groups like clans and moieties that, in turn, gave rise to elites making the process of choosing the favored easier and more acceptable. In turn, deities were created to bless the neat system. The holy ones were hailed and displayed with innumerable ceremonies and dances among the petroglyphs and pictographs decorating rocks on arroyo walls. Ceremonies have tended to have a monopoly on the time of human beings, whether they are held in kivas, temples, or sport stadiums.

The evolving proliferation of activities in the vista view is manifested at Gran Quivira II in the social organizing of the known world. The archeologists have labeled this early expression of manifest destiny as "regional integration." Chaco Canyon pueblos built in a large arroyo in Eastern Arizona related other communities from Colorado and New Mexico and southward into a great federation of people, including the Humanas at Gran Quivira. There is evidence for this reasonable assumption because Chaco organized the labor force and the governmental powers to build the largest kiva in the Southwest. It then followed that all roads led to and from "Rome" to touch and influence Gran Quivira and the neighboring pueblos, Abo and Quarai. Of course, these "roads" were pathways marked by finger- and toeholds chiseled in rock cliffs to facilitate the travelers, especially those with backpacks. Signal stations have been found along these ways and captivating petroglyphs to guide, to inspire, to educate, or to entertain the dog-tired walker. (See front map.)

If the forerunner Los Humanas village of Gran Quivira had only the hands, feet, and toes for packing, transporting, and distributing, they served well in their "regional integration" to carry salt, a hardier variety of corn, good beans, and the grey ceramics to trade for reddish ceramics, exotic bird feathers, and weaving crafts.

Los Humanas was a thriving society of largely unknown origins, but strongly influenced by Anasazi cultures, with permanent residences built like ancient Troy with one age constructing on the ruins of an earlier one. Their multi-purpose rooms, their aqueducts, their great churches called kivas where religion and government—just as in our modern day—were blended, were obvious evidence of the presence of "civilization" in the New World. What is more, the nosey archeologists and the antsy anthropologists suggest that the Humanas group lived in peace with its immediate neighbors and among those in its vast regional integration. Even the Apaches and Comanches, dreaded as they were by the more peaceful Pueblos and other Anasazi, were largely trading, not raiding. Something like the prophet Isaiah's dream of the holy mountain seemed to exist.

So, our second city, this one metamorphosed by the use of shining sandstone, was indeed larger than a pit village centuries earlier, but, like its predecessor, it suffered change and decay and collapsed to become derelict, another rocky carapace lying along the road of history.

Invading armies throughout history have brought destruction, slavery, suffering, and death, whether it be Joshua wiping out the children of Aii in biblical times or the Romans in classical times, or the pope's crusaders, or any of the modern nations whom John Steinbeck has described in his drama *The Moon is Down,* all were involved in the decivilizing process of war with its rape and mayhem. The invaders from Spain must be included. They forced the entrada on the Native Americans with the use of firearms, large animals, sailing ships, and "missions" to facilitate the finding and stealing of gold. In the last half century of the existence of Gran Quivira II, great suffering was brought on by oppression, social friction, degradation for those who oppress as well as those oppressed, desolation and disease, and, finally, dereliction and death. No structure remains, no infrastructure—only an extensive pile of rocks, ruins.

The rock mess is a grim reminder that one culture has imposed itself on another. The Spanish called their Coronados "frontiersmen," serving on "the northern frontier" of the Southwest to claim "free land" and to exploit. In so doing, one culture was imposed on a quite different one, resulting in a bicultural social order. This phenomenon was a result of the entrada, and made an impact upon, and a *modus vivendi* for the people of the Southwest. The Native Americans have suffered bitterly throughout the former colonial lands.

The geographical area which the authors have taken as Gran Quivira II has none of the earliest people extant. They long ago disappeared to leave the imposing temple in the "Humanas City" on the hill. The biculturalism is there, as is a Spanish cathedral to rival the imposing grandeur of the missions at nearby Abo and Quarai. Each structure rests heavily on buried kivas and homes of Indians. Although many people came from Spain and Mexico, no Latinos lived in the present town of Gran Quivira. For a new, northern European culture, the Anglos came from the east to create another frontier and to claim souls and gold nuggets at the same time. In this triculturalist setting may be found the story of the second part of the third Quiviran "city." The poet sings for our tale of the second village:

> Crumbling walls and fallen towers throw
>   their dismal, silent shadows.
> On the barren sandy desert, in the setting
>   evening sun
>   —Otto Goetz, "Gran Quivira,"
>   *New Mexico Magazine,* February 1934, p. 5

3

The Third Gran Quivira Emerges: End of the Nineteenth Century

The rise and fall of the third Gran Quivira, which existed roughly from 1875 to 1965, will be described in this section. Originally, the name "Gran Quivira," as we have indicated, seems to have come from the journeys of Coronado. It was called Grand Quivera at one time but now is known as Gran Quivira. Except for fleeting items in newspapers, almost nothing has been written about it. The early caretakers of the "ruins" on the hill hardly bothered to write notes about the village below and the people who lived in it. All who paused focused on the impressive grandeur of the homoscedastic piles of white limestone. Some were deeply affected by the impressive ruins but recorded little about them.

After the victories by the United States over Indians, Spanish, and Mexican people, the western impulse, with its sense of manifest destiny, used a generous homestead system to claim land in the New Mexico Territory. In an open clash with sheepherders, trappers, and gold seekers, Anglo homesteaders followed the trails widened with the flow of buckboards and conestogas. One of these trails from Texas intercepted a long-established one, first used by western Indians to connect pueblos east of the Rio Grande. Starting at Santa Fe, it passed to the south by several large pueblos and the valued salt flats. The Estancia Basin trail adjoining led eastward into what became Lincoln County and on southward into trade-minded Mexico. This route provided junctures where communities like Gran Quivira could be fostered.

The first person to come to this area to settle was Elisha Austin Dow (1849–1909) from Lincoln County, New Mexico. He proclaimed his land in the usual Spanish way, describing it extending from a designated cottonwood tree, across to a gulch, over to an "Ebenezer" of stones, and back to where he built his rugged rock shelter. He built his home about one-half mile west of the Gran Quivira "cathedral." It was constructed of rock and therefore cool by day and warm by night. This natural air conditioning was also provided by the rock ruins up on the hill, where many sheepherders, before the Anglo settlement, spent chilly nights.

It seems no one at that time valued the richness of nature in the area and later in the village. Thoughtlessly, it was called a barren land. However, not so to a boy of twelve (an author of this book) who recalls vividly how alive this "desert" was when his mother and ten-year-old sister and he lived in a one-room cabin near Lake Arthur, fifty miles southeast of Gran Quivira, for three months during the summer of 1920. They were completing the time required to prove the Homestead Grant for his older brother, an honored veteran with ribbons for the eight "major offensives" of the American Army in World War I. Here a wildcat could be heard shrieking at a pale dawn moon, like some woman in the throes of childbirth. Some days a pack of coyotes would yip near by. In the mornings and evenings, whippoorwills snatched from the air their last insect goody with a drawn-out peep interspersed with the buzzing vibration of their diving wings. Just before sunup, pygmy owls came to rest on a mesquite branch by the opening of a prairie dog hole. In addition to the ever-present pinyon and pine trees, there were useful plants like the yucca. The choice wood for fuel came from the roots of the mesquite, varieties of cacti, and a plant called by the natives "turpentine grass." It burned intensely, though green, and its smoke drove away clouds of large pinching ants that settled in their winged state on the cabin. Most

Elisha Dow, founder of Gran Quivira.

of these plants and animals had existed at Gran Quivira III, fifty years before, when Dow first came to the area.

Little did Elisha Dow know that he had settled on the top of pit villages that had been habitations over a thousand years before him. The problem still was water. In Dow's years, water was nearer the top of the ground. Wells were easier to dig. Still, according to his diary, water had to be "searched for." The soil was fertile, lacking only water.

This first settler in Gran Quivira was also the first of an educated, widely known, respected family that influenced Estancia Valley Chupadera slopes, and more. His father was Aaron Dow, a Quaker, who founded a college at College Springs, Iowa, and taught mathematics, Hebrew, and Greek. Elisha filed a homestead claim and made his living as a trader, peddling with a fleet of fifteen to twenty wagons up and down the valley trails from Gran Quivira to Chilili and beyond. Those who recall him say he was a tall, imposing man with a long black beard, rather like his ancestor, Lorenzo Dow, a peripatetic evangelist in New England who frightened people about the fires of hell unless they repented at once.[1] But the Gran Quivira Elisha Dow became a quiet, meditative Quaker, who played the accordion, enjoyed dancing, met and married Barbara McAfee, an Irish-Spanish woman of royal Spanish background, and attained some wealth in his widespread trading business.

Elisha had a deep concern for better human relations. He and "Barbarita" (the manner in which the Spanish people addressed Mrs. Dow) were the progenitors of a small international family made up of English, Irish, and Spanish, and eventually including the Methodist, Friends (Quakers), Baptist, and Catholic faiths.

Two sprawling letters of this pioneer are extant and give some sense of the character and value system of this unusual person. He addressed the New Mexico territorial governor, "His Excellency Governor L. Bradford Prince," at Santa Fe on July 2, 1889 (?), and on August 1 of the same year. The first letter, in July, appeals to the governor to see that the president of the United States, Benjamin Harrison, appoints more of "our native citizens" to offices in the territory. "Serious charges" already stand against two of three appointments made by the governor. "It is well known that the Democratic party did not ignore the native citizens" (Dow meant the Spanish) "nor the Catholic schools." This letter reveals that Dow spoke for and was identified with the Spanish people. Clara Corbin, another first settler who was of Victorian mien (more about her later), identified him as a "Mexican," a person to be paid for doing chores.

Dow's second letter pointed out other significant concerns. The area had economic possibilities. Fred Harvey, the founder of the famous hotels that were built in cities along the Santa Fe railroad line, was searching for Indian relics and pottery to sell to tourists during the long trip from Chicago to Los Angeles. Harvey's agents visited Indian dwellings and pueblos where all manner of rugs and pottery could be found to buy cheap and sell high. Archeologists at the Brooklyn Museum were also searching for Indian specimens for teaching aids for the museum. There were aggressive seekers for gold who were convinced that $17 million worth was buried near the walls of the Gran Quivira mission.

In this letter to Governor Prince, Dow continues to inform him about the many Indian-Spanish ruins from Chilili down to Tajique and Manzano, "more than any part of the Territory." "Still standing against the sky," he reports, "are the walls of Abo and Quarai, just as those at Gran Quivira." He offered to talk with the older men in the area to gather "a more correct account of these old ruins." He told him not only about gold, relic seekers, and the ancient structures, but also about the old apple orchards planted by the Spanish friars that continue to bear "apples in quantity."

The diary of this first citizen of Gran Quivira is owned by Ernest Garcia of Albuquerque, New Mexico. It covers only two and a half years (1885–87), yet it sheds additional light on Dow and his community. As the Yankee Clippers used ports of call, so

Clara Corbin, the enigmatic lady from Ohio who lived in the cathedral ruins.

his fifteen to twenty wagons moved from settlement to settlement, picking up deliveries and dropping them off elsewhere along the way or at their final destination. The diary mentions pelts and wool as common cargo, along with food items such as pheasants, potatoes, partially cut up "old cow," coffee, lard, corn, cheese, and antelope meat. Wire fencing was "peddled" too, causing increased acrimony between the sheepherder Mexicans and the new Anglo settlers seeping into New Mexico. English names of some new immigrants into the area of Dow's trade route are noteworthy: Humphrey, McAfee, McLean, Whitney, Hyder, Millis, and McIntosh, apparently chiefly English and Scotch-Irish people.

Diary entries tell of the popularity of certain activities: Sunday night dances that lasted well past one o'clock in the morning were mentioned. Chilili was the "playtown" where the dances were usually held. In later years when the Anglos were established at Gran Quivira (1920–1940), the "playtown" seems to have been at Claunch, nine miles southeast of Gran Quivira. Elisha Dow enjoyed instrumental music. He often commented on "spending time reading," or "at home reading." By 1887, Tajique now was his home, even though he operated one store in Gran Quivira and another in nearby Pinos Wells.

Religious activities were important, judging by entries such as "nine new members last Sunday," "began to read Bible through," and "picked two verses to memorize." Often there was no church building, so private homes were used. The intrepid Elisha, though not a priest, organized the town of Tajique to build a Catholic church. In gratitude, the Catholic townspeople insisted he be buried in front of the altar, even if this was traditionally the place for the priest. But, "No," objected the peripatetic salesman, Dow, pointing out that only a prelate could be there. However, his grave stands prominently outside the front doors of the little church.[2]

Quaker Dow had some other trouble with the church. The parish priest was intent on firing a teacher and Dow wrote, "I gave

The grave of Elisha and Barbarita Dow, which can be visited on a former busy wagon trail between Lincoln and Santa Fe, New Mexico.

that priest a hashing over about the school matter at Punta de Aqua." On Sunday, August 2, 1883, "I went to meeting to hear 'the protestant' tell falsehoods. We answered him in the evening." These frictions brought him into court. Both his brother-in-law McAfee and he were found guilty. The charges are unknown and because of a fire in the county building, will remain so. Inference might be used for an explanation. It would note that Dow, since his Lincoln County War days, seemed to support a just legal procedure in, for example, "hunting cattle" and in determining which animals were his and what to do with the unbranded critters claimed by more than one cowboy group.

His friends, all called Mexicans by the Anglos, were Bartoli Gonzalez, Viterli Luhan, and Antonio Chavez, who helped him build a dam. In another diary note, Ron Ortiz and Juan Chavez organized horse loaning among themselves at roundup times. They herded for others at $25 per month or $300 a year.

Dow was, according to his diary, involved in other communal activities which can be only mentioned: "taking the census of school children," "going prospecting for water," "writing letters to the newspapers and to politicians," and taking time to become one of the latter himself. He was a self-educated man who, for the most part, lived at ease in a clash of cultures brought to him by the intermarriage. There is little evidence that the Anglos ever really accepted the Dow family. At best, they only accommodated to it.

A fascinating person appeared in the community in these emergent years before a post office started in Dow's store, tantalizing because Clara Corbin was—according to both her picture and her actions—an educated, patrician-like, domineering lady, who had a severe handicap: blindness. She needed a rope to guide her to her outhouse and another to her clothesline. Clara A. B. Corbin asked "the Mexicans" to give her sheet-iron roofing to cover one of the little rooms of the hoary pueblo, and thus settled down to stay. Somewhere she had heard the gold story, millions of dollars tied up in Franciscan gold goblets and Spanish platters along with jeweled pieces buried somewhere nearby. Her husband, Mr. William G. Corbin, a Civil War veteran, could claim and pay for a homestead in addition to hers so after his death she would become the sole owner of all the land surrounding the gleaming monumental land of the second Gran Quivira. Any riches if found, would repay the blind woman for *costa* and much more.

Many others wished to own the ruins, but among the most active organizations were the Chicago Field Museum, the University of Pennsylvania, and several colleges in New York—Oswego, Buffalo, and Rochester, plus the Brooklyn Museum in New York City. Corbin was the first Anglo woman to visit and use her husband's veteran homesteading rights to file a claim (No. 4544) for the land upon which Gran Quivira II rested. Another Anglo woman, Virginia McClurg, who was employed by the Brooklyn Museum, wished to gain this valuable pueblo-mission for its archeological and educational possibilities. Her husband was a Civil War veteran also and could take advantage of homesteading rights. Here were two intelligent, vigorous, outdoor women vying with one another, in some ways somewhat questionable, to achieve the high goal of becoming the sole owner of the ruins of the city on the hill. McClurg argued in court that Corbin's claim was fraudulent because Corbin was not married to the veteran, and her declared intentions to farm the land weren't "sound," as required by homestead law. Corbin had to show, McClurg said, the desire "to make her claim a permanent home." Corbin could hardly reveal her real reasons for owning Gran Quivira: security for her blind old age and security while she wrote books which, once sold, would underwrite her search for gold. The Washington D.C. patent office ultimately upheld Corbin's claim. She believed the name should be Gran Quivira and that it was misnamed by some Hispanics who had come from the Rio Grande Valley. At the same time she changed her own name to Corbyn—substituting a *y* for *i*. This change was conjectured to be an attempt to stress her Welsh ancestry in the midst of "Mexicans."

Elisha Dow was considerate of Corbyn's many idiosyncrasies; he continued to dig wells for McClurg and for her and was paid $20 a month by Corbyn to stay on the land to "fight off squatters while she was away." For Corbyn to identify Dow as a "Mexican" tended to ensure trouble arising out of all efforts of that group to expropriate her treasured land. She had no good reason to alienate Dow, a first citizen of New Mexico.

Virginia McClurg lost her efforts to help turn the mission-pueblo into part of the archeology department of Brooklyn Museum. The "largest ruin in the Southwest," visited by the renowned Adolph Bandolier, was to have been used for gathering artifacts and as a place to hold classes in the summer months. McClurg fell in love with the stately walls and the pueblo city just as Corbyn had done. She wrote in July 1901 accurately and affectionately of the place while discussing "The Climate" in her report entitled, "The Pueblos of the Salinas."[3]

After these events, Clara Corbyn pitched a tent near the mission-pueblo and with an antique typewriter finished writing *La Gran Quibira: A Musical Mystery* and then started eighty-five pages of a sequel called *The Gates of Gaza*. Anyone reading a few pages of the mystical, exotic book will recognize the author to be highly educated and one who knew something of the major religions of the world. However, it is opaque writing, revealing a person suffering from delusions of grandeur and a vivid imagination. She interspersed her writing with typing letters for people living in the ruins. She did this for Ida Dow, who was Elisha's daughter, and the village's first postmistress.

Respect for Elisha Dow appears again in the history of Gran Quivira, as he reveals his concern for educating his children well. Ida had a private tutor from Connecticut, Anne Whitman, who later married Ida's cousin, Willie Down. Elisha then sent Ida to the Harwood Home Boarding School for Women in Albuquerque.

Ida Elizabeth Dow Garcia in late 1960's.

Ida Dow Garcia, daughter of Gran Quivira's founders, was its first postmaster. She was well educated, attractive, and competent.

She became known as a charming young woman around Gran Quivira who for fun rode pigs and who, in her teens, won a marathon dance with a young man, Roman Garcia, who later became her husband. Their first home was in the modern Gran Quivira at the foot of the hill, where they managed her father's store and where she was appointed postmistress—just the place for these two people, whose family backgrounds were of several national groups.[4] Gran Quivira, in this moment of its history, now bore a truly international complexion.

Clara, "the queer English lady," knew Ida, who helped her mail circulars for marketing her bizarre book. Before Ida's death in 1978, she left with her son, Ernest Garcia, a description of Clara Corbyn and her tent home in the ruins. Aristocrat though Corbyn was, she lived alone, too poor to hire a guide or an aide. Two windows, one on each side of the tent, provided light. A "Chick Sales" type of one-seater wood privy, the kind marketed by Sears Roebuck, with the famous slanted-up roof, was roughly fifty feet from the door. To the right of it was a clothesline. Cords ran from each into the tent to guide the blind woman to these necessities. According to Ida, Clara did her own cooking over a small wood stove. "We visited her," writes Ida, "about once a week and she was always clean and neat in her dress style." Her Victorian dress may have been her only one. "She had beautiful eyes, clear pink complexion and brown hair." She was robust-looking and seemed to get sufficient food. Soap and towels were around, near a "neatly kept bed." By her typewriter was a pile of typed sheets of paper to which she added constantly. Most of the content came from her dream world. Again, Ida: "We found her a solitary woman not talking of much except the weather or ordinary things. However, she was always glad to see us and would stop typing for a little chat."

This blind woman managed to get free rides with ranchers to the railroad station, where she argued with the conductor for a pass to Tucson, Arizona, or to Los Angeles, California. Up to the very end of her days she walked the streets of many western cities, lonely, more and more bedraggled, an object of pity. This arresting person, who once owned Gran Quivira and lived there off and on for twenty years, finally died in a Los Angeles charity hospital in 1908.

In this book, *The Tale of Three Cities*—"Three Gran Quiviras," as it might be called—the story of the third Gran Quivira can be divided roughly into two parts: The first begins in 1887, when the Dows arrived, and extends to 1912, when they and many of their "Mexican" friends moved to Tajique and Willard to live with other Spanish-speaking people. Those were the years highlighted by the important Irish-Spanish citizen Elisha Dow; his daughter, the sparkling postmistress, Ida; and the educated, eccentric Clara Corbyn. Tensions over homestead conflicts, rivalry between squatters, between cattle and sheep herders, and between intrusive Anglos versus "Mexicans," were the chief concerns of these decades.

It is well known in history that one city often builds on the rubble of an earlier one. Ancient Troy is the classic example. This pattern is also evident to visitors to Grand Quivira II. The big Indian pueblo reveals three or more layers of civilization below it. Therefore, one would not be surprised to read in the archives that the great beam over the doorway of the mission church was pulled down sometimes between 1896 and 1905 and it appeared at the side of Elisha Dow's rock house in Gran Quivira III! If vigas like this were taken away and reused, one can be sure the roughly dressed rocks of the sanctuary were put to use also. But the same activity occurred at Abo and Quari, where French and Mexican settlers are accused of borrowing. The archeologist John Ivy believes that removal of the vanishing lintel beams over the sacristy at Gran Quivira resulted in the collapse of walls, and estimates this destruction as taking place between 1896 and 1905.

Notes

1. The story is told that Lorenzo Dow claimed if the devil was around he could confront him and drive him out of souls or their homes. One night he stopped at a farmer's home in Maine and was put to bed in the hay loft. Soon he was awakened by a lover carrying on with the farmer's wife in the kitchen below him. The farmer was heard returning home and his wife advised her lover to hide in the big lint basket beside the fireplace. Things went well until the Rev. Dow bestirred himself and climbed out of the loft shouting, "The evil is in this house and I can prove it." With tongs, he threw a hot spark into the flammable lint. With a flare of fire the lover ran away as Lorenzo shouted, "Who doubts I can drive out devils?"
2. This incident was given to us by an old resident; it is not in the diary.
3. It was not with a feeling of ease that McClurg agreed to let "Old Kleber" (Cleever?), a German who claimed land that included some of the northern portion of this largest pueblo-church combination in the vast Rio Grande valley, to take her in his heavy baggage wagon down to Gran Quivira from Albuquerque and return. "Old Kleber" was an unofficial first custodian of Gran Quivira since circa 1903 who had been protecting the constructions and who showed people around. For the six-day trip he provided his scholarly passenger with his aluminum drinking cup! He took McClurg's picture among the ruins but when he brought on board his wagon a foundling coyote pup, he declined to uncover it for a photo, saying coyotes couldn't stand hot sun. No matter how much McClurg might wish to move faster on the trip, the well-cared-for horses were never urged to trot. Kleber would pause most anytime to provide them with green grass and cool water. Their comfort took precedence over any passenger—therefore, hot sun for six days!
4. In passing, Ida Dow informs us on the farm activity before the bean production rage, beginning about 1913 to 1914. The young Garcia's had two Jersey cows that provided milk and butter. With them were four horses, a flock of chickens, and enough milk and eggs that they were able to give some to sheepherders in exchange for mutton.

4
Politics, Peanuts, Piety

The second half of the story of the last Gran Quivira encompasses two world wars; the flood of pinto beans to feed the Allies warring in Europe; the coming of the railroad; the rise of a nationwide religious movement which in the Southwest was at this time centered in the Gran Quivira area; and last but not least in importance,

Bean harvester relics of the great bean boom around Gran Quivira. From their parts, Gordon McMath made junk sculpturing that pleased the *Smithsonian Magazine* editor.

the emergent concern of people in the West to protect the remnants of ancient Native American civilization, stretching back more than half a millennium, a concern that culminated in development of the National Park System. Many persons then and even now would not believe that these early Southwesterners built several-storied structures well before the arrival of Columbus. The impulse to learn more about the earliest occupants and to preserve their artifacts—from shard fragments to houses—has brought university scholars and national park rangers to Gran Quivira even to the present day.

The second half of this story is dominated by the Anglo-Americans filtering into the Manzano, Estancia, and Chupadera areas just east of the broad Rio Grand valley. They came in ever greater numbers after 1914, enticed by the generous homesteading laws. The trickle became a tide and the Native American population retreated, as did the Hispanic sheepherders. Many of the latter, like the Tenorios, the Garcias, the Salases, and the Dows, settled in the Hispanic villages of Tajique and Chilili on the east side of the Manzano Mountains or presided over large sheep- raising ranches. As a result, almost all the older people living in the Gran Quivira community since World War I were Anglos whose fathers filed 160-acre homestead claims up and down the Chupadera valley.

The homesteaders established tiny settlements and started schools in almost each township. These tiny crossroad school settlements were given colorful names like Cedarvale (a place that accepted a traveler overnight with free food for himself and his draft animals), Liberty, Penos Wells, Center Point, X-ray (a name brought from Texas), Stinking Springs (due to sulphurous waters), and a larger community named Claunch.

On the pinyon and juniper plain, 6,000 feet above sea level, bustling economic activities marked principally sheep raising and some cattle ranching, which were slowly overcome by a single crop: the pinto bean, which had found itself in great demand in

World War I. Since then, a few Anglos seemed to return to cattle ranching. A monotony settled over this bleak land that was burned out by heat waves and misuse of the land, motivated by greedy cultivators. The only excitement was "the ruins," luring gold diggers on one hand and scholars on the other. One group was intent upon discovering the secrets of the white rock cathedral and the other fixed on stealing gold, as Cortes had done in the fifteenth century and as the oil pirates are now in the twentieth.

How would one describe the community of Gran Quivira III, whose first settler was Elisha Dow? Sociologists seem to have two chief distinguishing features: (1) demarcated earth space and (2) inhabitants who commune regularly. The space of the larger community (see map on p. ii) of Gran Quivira III, in which is nestled the village, began on Route 55 at Mountainair, New Mexico, proceeding southeast, passing the Garrison ranch, and reaching to include the acreage of Vernie Wells (who was an early governmental protector of the sacred walls). (Note map on p. ii.) Before turning the corner of the Wells ranch, Grand Quivira Community extends to include the last community member, Sylvia Lewis, whose mother was among the first Anglo homesteaders and who always kept an eye on White Oak Cemetery.

Proceeding southward on Route 55 from the Wells ranch is the Connell ranch—and they, like others, say, "We live in Gran Quivira." On southward is the ranch of H. C. Fulfer, whose father acquired a homestead nearby and served for several years as caretaker of the "ruins." As one proceeds southward, one reaches the historic Gran Quivira, where the post office and the Dow home were located and where now only three or four citizens live, most notably Mr. and Mrs. Jack Kite. Mrs. Kite's father operated a large general store in the village and these octogenarians were our chief informants.

Gran Quivira III was a type of "line community," as were many towns and cities in the Southwest. It was strung and sprawled along an auto/truck road. East and west of Route 55 are people who say, "I don't live in Gran Quivira." These "erratics," who visit friends and relatives often, perhaps to attend church, are few and far between. At death they may use the White Oaks Cemetery of the Quivirans or other communities, but they are not part of the group that kept the White Oaks Cemetery neat and weeded. However, although nearly twenty-five miles from the railroad in Mountainair, most families say they live in Gran Quivira despite the fact that this community no longer officially exists.

A spur of Route 55 runs a half-mile uphill to Gran Quivira III, now renamed Salinas Pueblo Mission National Monument. Here are today the spectacular multiple abodes, many still buried in the dust, of the Anasazi—"the ancient ones," as the Indians have labeled these earlier people.

The only institution surviving the decaying village of Gran Quivira is the church, the Assembly of God, and its remaining inhabitants are members. It is a potent centering factor for the community, just as the Catholic cathedrals were for the Spanish communities of Abo and Quari. "Real" Gran Quivirans are almost always buried in the White Oaks Cemetery.

The present-day visitor will find only the Old and New Assembly of God church buildings, the Jack and Louise Kite home (built in 1970), a couple of frame houses on the hill, and the remnants of the gas station in front of the Turner store. Other buildings remain, and some of them are identifiable.

The main street of Gran Quivira ran north and south, parallel to the present Route 55. (See map on p. iii.) This street was two or three city blocks long and encompassed the high school, the Assembly of God church, the grade school, the teachers' homes, the barber shop, the large Turner store and gas station, and several homes. Over time there were seven stores in Gran Quivira. At the peak of prosperity, during the war years (1904–1963), there were three general stores, three grist mills, a dentist's office, the rock house of the barber, a schoolhouse, a high school, the Assembly of God church, and the post office. An automobile garage was at one time a part of Turner's General Store, which seemed to supply every necessity. At various times the park custodian lived in the village, starting with W. H. "Doc" Smith, custodian from 1923–1936.

During the life of this village, water was provided by as many ways as possible, including sixty cisterns that caught rain for later use, some shallow and several deep-drilled wells, and an inadequate spring from which came a little water. The Indians of the area had once carted water on their backs from the Gallinas Mountains. It is doubtful that the Anglo inhabitants of Gran Quivira did this as well, but we do know they purchased water hauled to them in 200-gallon tanks, a system used to this day. Inhabitants living in this area have drilled wells (600 feet deep) and the water can be used with the application of modern softeners and additives.

There were some 800 citizens in this historic community. (See map on p. iii.) Several stores served the inhabitants from time to time. Those with the longest existence were Miller's Store (owned by Diamond Tooth Miller); Scribner's Store, which burned down and not a trace exists now; J. P. Maples and Sons, who seemed collectively to enjoy fisticuffs; and the leading and largest one, Jones Turner (Louise Kite's father), which sold a variety of provisions and had an adjoining blacksmith shop on the northwest corner and a modern (for those years) gasoline station out of the front door.

The Miller and Turner stores served as social centers. Miller's store had small tables with colorful cloths where drinks and casual food were served and dominoes and other games were played. Croquet was played in the yard and discussions were carried on about the baseball teams organized in several neighboring centers in the valley. The "spit and argue club" of older men met informally each morning but didn't chew tobacco (except Diamond Tooth Miller) because the Assembly of God forbade it. The area was strongly pro-Democratic and populist wisdom was evident in all directions. This wisdom was ardently new Deal. Franklin Roosevelt was a national hero and Senator Chavez was the progressive senator to be supported. This was true of "Anglo" and "Mexican" citizens. Settlers like the Tenorios, Salases, and Dows were English and Irish but because of intermarriage with Spanish were identified incorrectly (if one must "label" so freely) as "Mexicans" or perhaps "Spanish" in the local social pecking orders. They were united in their support for the Democratic party. In the FDR years, although the two ethnic groups were, due to population spread and keener economic competition, just beginning to create sharper geographic borders and cultural identifications, they were voting together for New Deal policies. No Native Americans were members or other ethnic groups to complicate the village population more. The only exception was one Black man who lived on "nigger hill," some miles south of Mountainair, on the border of the community of Gran Quivira.

Political leaders from the village were vigorous and colorful frontiersman, and as New Mexico, following Arizona, was becoming the last stand of our "moving frontier," we may so identify them. The several prominent store owners were strongly political like the pioneer Elisha Dow before them. Dow was well known from Gran Quivira north to Santa Fe. Dean Whitford Miller, or "Diamond Tooth," grinned intentionally, some thought to expose his tooth and to win larger elections with mouthings of intriguing brilliance. J. P. Maples, the owner of J. P. Maples and Sons and the man who had founded the Gran Quivira Mercantile Co., was elected and reelected sheriff in the '30s. He is reported to have been crude and somewhat of a roughneck. Doubtless some Quivirans feared him and his bullying sons.

Merchant Jones Turner provided goods and services to the community from a larger building whose broken-down walls stand bleakly today against the prairie light. This respected man was an advocate of Franklin Roosevelt's ideas and served on political bodies to implement them. However, when the National Recovery Act (NRA) came in, things grew too complicated and he sold his store. Nevertheless, his store was the first to have electric lights, a blessing from the Rural Electrification Authority (REA) in 1937.

His daughter, Mrs. Louise Turner Kite, and her husband, Jack Kite, as has been pointed out still live in Gran Quivira. Jack, who always remained a Democrat, represented the party well in the progressive New Deal years and later made community changes by chairing or serving on important committees. Since Mrs. Kite had always lived in the village, she could reconstruct the street layout, just where the stores were including the barbershop, the teachers' homes, the school, the grannywomans' home, the grist mills, the roving family-to-family post office, and many of the departed and deceased.

The great influx of Anglo homesteaders seeking free land and a healthful climate resulted in a great deal of homogeneity in the village. Most of the Anglos had endured hardship before coming to New Mexico. They were not refugees in the modern sense; however, they had left familiar homes, families, and communities. They were not foreign-born but shared the camaraderie of being foreigners in New Mexico, which caused them to unite and develop community values.

As the original attractions of land and climate were somewhat well established, the European World War I added others—the task of supplying food for the doughboys of France appealed to patriotic feeling and provided the opportunity to make a good living. Homestead land was bought and sold and farms consolidated because 160 acres was hardly enough for a farmer to make a good living. In our interviews, we found only one rancher who stayed with cattle while all his neighbors in the community went wild over bean farming.

Mountainair became the shipping point for the region, giving it the identification "Bean Capital of the World." Since Gran Quivira village was only twenty-five miles south of Mountainair, it became a supply station for bean farmers, workers, and families.

Jack Kite, a caretaker of U.S. national parks.

Louise Turner Kite, wife of Jack, helped Mrs. Link identify persons who once lived in stone foundations that now barely protrude from ground level.

King Bean demanded full attention and people "ate beans baked, boiled, in salad and chili, stewed, and in soup." Chili originally was made without red beans in the Southwest, but now they are as acceptable as they were for the doughboys. Bean Day was an annual event when the sharecropper farmers came out in wagons and the owners appeared in buggies to celebrate a crop that might produce at the elevator 600 to 1,000 hundred-pound sacks of beans a day. Beans turned Gran Quivira III village from rags to riches. The boys, when girls were not present, yelled a marching couplet brought home by soldiers in World War I: "Beans, beans, the musical fruit, makes your ass go toot-di-toot." The demise of the pinto bean reversed this amazing farming process and within a mere thirty-five years, its absence left land and people devastated.

To summarize another way, the bean harvest provided the power to launch the rapid rise of the third city in this tale. Will an-

Mountainair, the "Bean Capital of the World," has a railroad station which remains unused.

other dramatic social or physical phenomenon produce another Gran Quivira population center?

In all the years from the original settlers of trade, then the cattle and sheep raising and the bean and the decline of Gran Quivira III, the hard-working and courageous people created outstanding institutions—schools and the Assembly of God church, post office and ordinary service institutions such as stores, a barber, a dentist—and simple social lives. Schools were established and maintained. Efforts were made to have a good curriculum and modern equipment, attract sturdy teachers, and maintain the interest and cooperation of parents. The church was active all day on Sundays, at weekly prayer meetings, and in daily lives. Singing and musical activities were organized, emphasized, and enjoyed. More and more interest and knowledge of the "ruins" started and began to be appreciated.

Because of the necessity to do for themselves and help others, there was no overt violence reported in newspapers or by informants. The one murder in this area (1923) was caused by a cattle dispute. There was little interaction between the Anglo and Mexican peoples and therefore only minimal accommodation of the Hispanic citizens or acknowledgment of their history. Many, if not most, communities a century ago felt comfortable only with their own kind and saw little need to include "others" into their social circle. This can become a silent majority of drawing circles.

5

The Valley Is Still There
By Gordon L. McMath,
Citizen of the Third City

The following homespun account entitled "The Valley Is Still There" was written by Gordon L. McMath, with contributions from Mrs. McMath. Beginning in 1929, they reared a family on a pinto bean farm adjacent to the Gran Quivira valley. The manner in which the McMaths describe their arduous life and that of their neighbors is realistic and full of localisms, and adds vitality to the social patterns in the preceding chapter. They wrote when the singular bean success was ebbing and thus have preserved an important time segment of American life that enhances vista perspectives. We have wondered why this serendipity in our West has escaped the sharp eyes of cultural historians in particular.

Before thanking the McMaths for giving us permission to present their little typescript booklet as chapter 5 in our book—co-authors with us—we wish readers to know that Mr. McMath is a recognized artist. He uses rusting metal from derelict bean threshers, wagon parts, and motors lying in the scrubby gramma grass, resting never far from the bleached cattle bones beloved of Georgia O'Keefe, and turns them all into the unfortunately named "junk art." See the Smithsonian *magazine for April 1995 (see pages 140–151) where several pictures in color of the author, his spouse, and his outdoor sculpture may be seen. We are most grateful to these friends who once lived in the great bean lands with the Jack Kites.*

Preface

This story is dedicated to all those folks and their descendants that had a part in this.

A special thanks to Donna, my daughter, for getting it all organized.

Thank you, Freeda Walker Brown, for the contribution of three of your poems.

I, Gordon L. McMath, was born at Mountainair, March 13, 1923, and spent most of my life in the Estancia valley.

This work is fictionally based on facts. I hope you enjoy and understand it.

Writing as if I were Capilla Peak is the only way that I could describe the Valley.*

The Valley Is Still There

I, Capilla Peak, am the second highest peak on the Manzano mountain range in central New Mexico. I look southeast out over a large valley 3,000 feet below.

The valley is about forty miles north to south and twenty east to west. On the extreme east side are a series of salt lakes where all the runoff water is captured and evaporates. In the past, this whole area was covered with water. Huge animals roamed the land as the water disappeared. The valley slowly evolved through several droughts and rainy seasons into a grassy plain with antelope, buffalo, and wild horses roaming the valley. The Indian came over the mountain from the west to hunt his winter meat, thereby discovering the salt lakes.

---

*Capilla Peak is immediately north of Gran Quivira area and east of the Chupedera hills. (Footnote contributed by EPL.)

The average rainfall is about twenty-one inches per year. Some years it is a lot more and others none at all. The grass is called gramma grass and will lie dormant if there is no moisture.

Some Catholic priests came up from Mexico and tried to convert the Indians. They built a large fort and church to the south called Gran Quivira and another closer into the south called Quarai and another west of there called Abo. After some years there was another drought that forced them to leave or starve to death.

After this drought broke, a few Spaniards started to come up from Mexico. They formed small villages along the foothills and farmed beans, corn, and garden produce. The Spanish government gave each family a land grant to graze their stock on and to farm. There are five of these; Punta, Manzano, Torreon, Tajique, and Chilili. A pony express rider came through from north to south or visa versa south to north each week to bring the mail from El Paso through Gran Quivira to Santa Fe.

Each town built a Catholic church of rather large dimensions for the times and each one is built on the same pattern, although not the same size. They are built in the form of a cross. It appears that one priest serves all the churches in the area, going from town to town on a donkey.

These people have a fiesta every fall to celebrate the harvest. Everything revolves around the church, even to the government and law. They are not a very highly educated people at this time, but they are a very happy people and whatever the priest says goes without question.

I am beginning to see another class of people show up in the valley. They are of a lighter complexion and speak a different language from the first ones here. They call themselves Anglos. Some of these people are downright mean, taking advantage of the Mexicans, killing, raping, and stealing. They started a newspaper called the *Gringo and the Greaser.* Mostly they just agitated and caused turmoil. Finally someone killed the editor and put a stop to that.

Also coming up from the south are some sheep ranchers with land grants for large holdings in the valley. The country has not been surveyed and there are boundary disputes all over. Everyone is carrying a gun and trying to protect his holdings or gain more. There are several range wars going on. Water is a problem for them as there are only a few springs and the creeks do not run all summer. Therefore, whoever controls the water controls the land. There are two large ranches, one at Estancia Spring and another at Antelope Springs, with several smaller ranches to the south.

There have been some outlaws coming over the mountains from the west and raiding and killing. This is a wild and lawless land but the future looks bright and the people have hope that everything will work out. They say next year will be better; the U.S. will take over and then we will have law. This became known as the "land of Mañana."

One spring morning when the air was clear and I could see far to the east, I saw some wagons with canvas sheets covering them come over the hills east of the salt lakes and make their way slowly to the west. Some of the wagons contained women and children while others had various kinds of machinery and large saws.

They proceeded right on up to the mountain canyon and set up camp. They drug out their machinery and set up a sawmill to make lumber from the ponderosa pine growing here. If I didn't miss count, there were eighteen different sawmills in these mountains before it was over.

I had been interested in what was going on here in the mountains and hadn't noticed much out in the valley, so when I did look at Capillo Mountain, I could see another group of people coming across the salt lakes. They proceeded to about seven miles out from the mountains and a little to the south, right out in the middle of the bald prairie by a large tree cactus, and set up permanent camp there. There was in this group one older man, one middle-aged fellow, one small child, three women, and two teenaged boys. They dug a hole in the ground and built up on the sides of the hole and moved in a small stove and one bed into this hole.[1] Then they went to the sawmill and got lumber to put a roof over this house they called a half dugout. The older fellow said, "Next year we will build a nice house."

Now, while several other families are coming in from the east and setting up camp from the north end of the Valley to the south end of the mesa, I went down to eavesdrop on these folks and to try to see what they were up to. Here is what I heard them saying.

"The first thing we have to do is get some water. I think we should write Uncle Jake and get him to come out here and bring his well drill. I bet he could get a lot of wells to drill if he gets water here. My forked stick says that he should strike water about 125 to 150 feet down. This hauling water from Punto is getting old."

I heard the wife say, "Lester, what are we going to do with this cottonseed? It is getting damp and moldy in this half dugout."

"We will put it in one of the wagons until next spring, when we will plant it," he said. "I sure hope someone puts in a cotton gin around here. I bet we can make a half bale to the acre easy. We will put this flat place in west of the house first and next year we will put in all of that flat ground to the south there. It sure is good to be able to just plow up the ground and not have to clear it and grub the stumps before we can get it into production. Ma, I think we should write Uncle Andy and tell him about this land over southeast of here and try to get him to come on out before all the good land is taken. I sure hope we don't have any trouble with that sheep man over in the draw there. He has been grazing his sheep over this way every year. We may have to put up a fence around our farmland."

I am back on top of the mountain now. I see a black smoke and a lot of people working like ants. The A.T. & S.F. Railroad is building a line through the valley. It appears that it will go west through the canyon where the priest has the gold mine. They are drilling for water on the right of way just west of the salt lakes.

Things are happening so fast around here that it is hard to keep up with it all. They have started a town down there where the spring is. It is called Estancia, and several people live there. They are starting a general store called the Valley Supply. The railroad has come through the salt lakes and ends at a small town called Willard. They are building on west to a town called Mountainair at the top of the divide. A railroad is being started in the south at Torrance, where it begins and proceeds to Willard and through Estancia and on north to Santa Fe. This railroad is the New Mexico Central.

Some two or three years have passed since I visited the settlers out on the flats, so we will go back and see what is going on. They had drilled a well and sure enough, water—and good water— appeared at 130 feet. They have put up a windmill and tank and are so proud of it. But in the time that has passed, the government has come in with a survey and opened the whole country up for homesteading. Each person is entitled to 160 acres of farmland or 640 acres where it is only fit for grazing. Now, these folks that had come in early and filed on their quarter-section (160 acres, that is) found that they had misjudged where the property line would be and had built and drilled their well on another person's homestead. "But so what? Next year when we make a good crop, we will build a nice house and drill a well over on our land."

Nearly every train that comes in has two or three families with all their livestock, equipment, and household goods to homestead on land. They bring their seed and plants to establish their farms. Some have enough money to build a house and barn while others have to live in a tent or half- dugout. The weather continues to be moderate and dry, so really it isn't too bad.

There seems to be a lot of sick folks coming here for the dry air. In fact, one fellow, who they brought in on a stretcher to the top of the mountains over north of here on the Bosque, has set up a goat ranch and is selling cheese on the big river to the west. He has recovered from his lung sickness and is able to work now.

Now nearly all the land has been taken and there is some kind of dwelling on every quarter- section. Most of the farms north of the A.T. & S.F. Railroad have drilled a water well and have good water. The water south of the tracks is gyp (a local term for artesian—gypsum—well water, usually containing sulphur) and very hard to locate. Lots of dry holes have been drilled. The people living south haul their water from Willard or Moutainair down to Gran Quivira. They also dig cisterns near their house and catch the rainwater off the roof. The mesa doesn't have a natural drain as the valley does, and therefore there are several basins that catch rainwater for the livestock. Not all of the mesa land is good farmland and most of it has cedar and piñon growing that have to be cleared away to farm it. The soil is very rich and sandy.

Andy had come out and gone back after he saw how the cotton crop was coming along. He sure kidded them about trying to raise cotton where the last frost in the spring is in May and the first in the fall is in September. They should know that in the South it took thirteen months out of the year to make a cotton crop.

The old gentleman had been talking to the Spanish up in the hills and they told him to plant pinto beans and Mexican corn if he wanted to make a crop. That is what he had been doing the past years, and had been doing very well. I heard him tell one of the others that as he rode across country the other day to file his records on the homestead, the grass was up to his stirrups in the big draws. Now, this family had five grownups in it, so they were entitled to that many quarter-sections. And they were able to file on adjoining quarters to make a rather sizable farm.

I must leave them and take a look at what is going on in the rest of the country.

Most of the homesteaders are all in about the same condition. Water is the biggest problem for all of them, it seems. In the towns (now, you will forgive me, but I just barely can see Buford on the north and Claunch on the south, so I will just tell you of the towns that I can see best), it looks like Willard is the most progressive and has the best opportunity to be a thriving town. It has twenty-nine saloons and several dance halls, a bank, and two big general stores where you can buy anything from lace to a coffin. Several hundred—maybe over a thousand—people live here. They tell me that down south of Willard a town called Torrance was the county seat, where the courthouse was a boxcar. They have moved it to Estancia and now that is the county seat.

Estancia has the railroad yards and three or four hotels It also has a couple of general stores and two rather large bean cleaners and warehouses for the storage of pinto beans (c. 1917).

Mountainair, on the Santa Fe Railroad, is growing a little slower than the other towns, as water is a problem there. On the other hand, it is doing better as they have a Chautaugua, which is an assembly for education and entertainment by lectures, concerts, etc. Mountainair would like to be the cultural center of the valley. They passed a law that there would be no dance halls in town or liquor sold there.

They have five very large bean warehouses and became known as the "Pinto Bean Capital of the World." They have five or more large general stores and the largest hardware in the valley. The farmers can buy all their farm supplies and machinery here.

It looks good out in the valley. The people have built a one-room school in nearly every township where there are enough children to warrant it and, of course, they have built a school in every town, including those that were here before the homesteaders came. The sheep man and rancher are being squeezed out and the dirt farmers have taken over the whole valley. Some of the farmers have a few beef cows and a milk cow for sure. All of them have chickens and pigs, and raise a garden to help feed the family, but pinto beans have become the main diet of these people.

I overheard one man from out on the mesa say that if he could get his wife to go along with it he was going to put in four hundred acres of beans out there next year on that flat. He said they were the easiest thing to raise that he ever saw. "All you have to do is go out there, live in a tent in the summer (as there is no water available there), and plant your beans in May and harvest them in September, bring them into the elevator and they will give you at least three dollars and maybe five dollars a sack (one hundred pounds). Now, it is nothing at all unusual to get ten sacks to the acre and at five cents a pound and four hundred acres, that's more money than I am able to figure. Anyway, I think I can get a loan from the bank to buy the feed and seed."

Another man said, "You better go easy on that, you may not get five cents a pound—and then what?"

Estancia Valley Winds

Sweeping downward from the mountains,
    out across the fertile land
Ever changing in the volume,
    of its load of moving sand.
Hurling ever onward, eastward
    shrieking with a demon's glee,
Wrecking all within its pathway,
    damage that no eyes can see.
Human hands cannot control it,
    ruthless, making no amends,
Only bent upon destruction . . .
    that's the Estancia Valley winds.

—Freda Walker Brown

These winds were equally fierce in the adjacent Chupadera Valley, southward.

I must stop here and explain to you about farming beans on

this land. This valley is largely covered with a heavy growth of gramma grass and to cultivate it you must plow it up and break up the sod into a mulch. The land is a sandy loam and will grow nearly anything that the season will allow. When they farm beans on the land they take all of the crop off and leave a sandy flat mulch without any straw or other material to hold the soil.

The bean thrasher is set up near the field and the beans, vine and all, are hauled out of the field to it. The hull and vine, after the beans have been removed, are valuable for cow feed.

The beans are put into sacks, taken to the elevators, re-cleaned, and weighed. The elevator buys the beans at the established price.

I don't wish to go into what went on at the elevators, as it is somewhat of a secret. I do know that the poor farmer is left at the mercy of the elevator operator. All they can do is take their beans to them and hope for the best and take whatever price they offer. There sure is a lot of grumbling and griping, but not a thing they can do, as most of them have a note or grocery bill to pay off and need the money bad.

Now to the fellow who was to plant four hundred acres next year. He did get the loan and purchased his feed and seed and moved out there in March. He took with him twelve head of good work stock and broke out his sod land in good shape. No rain fell, as often happens in this country. From where I am here on the top of the mountain, I cannot see the field that he plowed up, but I can see a large dust cloud off down that way that never was there before.

The Rise and Fall of the Dry-Land Pinto Bean

Long ago the homesteaders
Found that they must plow and plant,
And they were the kind of people
Ones who never said "I can't."

Found the seeds that grew the best
Were the native pinto beans,
Never thought that it would flourish,
Far beyond their wildest dreams.

It was known as dry-land farming,
All they needed was the rain,
That kept falling in the seasons
To raise beans, and feeds, and grains.

Soon the beans became their mainstay
Need necessary tools,
Came the tractors, trucks, and threshers,
Next recleaners—then bean pools.

Giant buildings were erected,
Then new bean sacks were unfurled,
With the proud claim of the business,
"The Bean Capital of the World."

This the peak of the proud pintos,
Thinking back you will recall,
When the great drought swept the valley,
And there was no more rainfall.

They must turn to other methods,
Irrigation came in view,
As they planted, they would harvest,
It was all so very new.

Learned they were not dry-land pintos,
All who cooked them soon found out,
But the corn, the cane, alfalfa,
Brought more profit, without doubt.

All that's now left of the pintos
Are the memories of the past,
Vacant buildings, bean machinery,
Gains that were too good to last.

There may, never be, in history,
You may, never see again,
The short era of bean farming . . .
By those brave homesteading men.

—Freda Walker Brown

    The people in the valley have their land ready to plant but there just isn't enough moisture to sprout the seed. One fellow that I have been watching had been working in Mountainair at the lumberyard. He managed to trade a small house that he had built for a wagon and team of little red mules. His brother and he rented a farm and have enough moisture to plant on. As the beans come up, they just stand there with two leaves pointing up to the sky praying for rain. Day after hot day passed without a cloud in the heavens. The hot wind blows and the beans die. The brother that had come to help farm joins the army to fight the Kaiser in WWI. The other, with his wife and small child, finds a temporary job at the rock crusher on the west side of the mountains.

    People out in the valley are doing everything they can to save their stock for next year. They burn the spines off the cactus so the cows can eat them. They grub the bear grass or soap weed and chop it in small pieces, trying to get the stock to eat that. There is a little salt grass growing in the lower valley around the salt lakes. Several of the farmers drive their horses and mules down there, hoping they will find enough to eat to get them through until next year. Three feet of snow finally breaks the drought at Thanksgiving time.

    The fellow that had a job at the rock crusher came back to the valley to stay with his in-laws. He is a very sick man with the flu. In nearly every house in the valley someone is sick and often everyone that lives there is sick in bed with the flu. The snow outside is up over the fence posts and the temperature is near zero all the time. Lots and lots of people die and they are not able to bury them because they can't get to the cemetery and the ground is frozen two feet deep. The ones that are able take a few boards off the side of the barn or wherever they can get them. Then they build a coffin and put the dead ones out in the snow bank until they can get them buried. The snow has the ground covered until after Easter in the spring.

Of course, you can guess what is happening to the livestock that were already starving for feed.

Hopefulness

It isn't raining rain to me,
It's raining pinto beans.
It's filling cracks in empty sacks,
And you know what that means.

So do not fuss about the wind,
Or dark clouds hanging low,
Because it means there'll be more beans
To pay up what we owe.

—Freda Walker Brown

When the farmers get into town with a team and sleigh, I hear them say, "Boy, next year is going to be good. I sure hope the banks can get some more financing because we are going to need it come next year. I think I will put in every acre I have in beans. If I can make a good crop I am going to sell out and go back to where I came from."

Another said, "I can tell you one thing, I ain't going to get caught in this fix again. Next year I am going to get in plenty of wood from the mountains and I am going to plant half of my land in feed. There ain't no use of that livestock suffering so."

Another said, "If you had the whole place in feed last year you wouldn't have been any better off. I tried that milo we used to raise one year and it looked good except the frost got it in the fall. I may grow some wheat next year. I wonder if it will grow here."

Spring came at last with the birds singing and the flowers blooming, the sun shining bright and warm every day. In the language that I have, there just isn't proper words to describe this spring.

The fields are lying fallow and ready for the plow, with plenty of moisture to bring forth a bountiful crop. The beans and corn are planted and spring out of the ground, growing and blooming at a fantastic rate. They are getting showers and rains every few days and it looks good for this year. On the 10th of July a big black cloud formed in the northwest and such lighting and roaring you never heard or saw. It came down out of the north with a terrible wind and noise, traveling south very fast. It was only about a mile wide but it left six inches of hail and destruction in its wake.

Next day I heard the farmer that had talked about planting wheat telling the manager of the trading company that the hail had got him, but maybe it was a blessing as he was a wheat farmer and if they would carry him he would order seed and put the whole thing in wheat. The manager said he would have to talk to Mr. Illfield (the owner) about it. I heard him tell the secretary that they would have to go along or lose a lot of money.

It is coming on fall now and everyone is scurrying around trying to line up a harvest crew. The Mexicans in the small towns are anxious to work but do not have transportation. The going wage is a dollar fifty and lunch for a "can to can't day"—or a dollar a day and board. I heard one farm wife say she had learned that the Mexes would eat beans three times a day, so she had them for breakfast along with eggs and biscuits and the only ones that ate beans were her two teenage boys.

The crops are good this year; nearly all the beans are going C.R.C. (Choice recleaned). The elevators are full and beans are stocked outside on the sidewalks. The price is okay, too, as the war in Europe is winding down. But it seems to me that the farmer should get more than the elevator. The farmers that were in the path of the hail said, "Just wait until next year, then we will make it."

Very few want to sell out and go back where they came from now. It looks too good here. "Next year we will put in more, then you will see."

"I wish I could talk to them and warn them, but I am only a mountain and the only thing I can do is look down on them and feel sorrow for their plight and misfortune.

Year after year passes with little or no rain or snow. Some years there would be a small crop and others they couldn't even plant. In fact it has been ten years since the last good crop and here it is the great stock market crash and people all over the U.S. going hungry. The rains fell just right this year and a bumper crop of beans raised. Let us go down and see what the people are saying and doing now.

"I traded one hundred sacks of beans for a new six-cylinder Chevrolet. I would have gotten a Ford but that newfangled distributor on top of the motor will never work, so I got a Chevy. What do you think of the new Farmall tractor? Some say that a tractor will pack the ground so hard that nothing will grow. Sure would be nice not to have to feed a bunch of horses and mules through the winter. I may try to get me one. I understand there is a John Deere dealer in Estancia. I think I would rather have an Oliver Hart Parr out there on the mesa where we live. The land is sandy and all the equipment is in front of the drive wheels. I don't believe they would get stuck so easy."

"No, you are all wrong. I saw a Case [tractor] down in Texas with a four-row planter on it. That's the kind to have. If I had one of them I could farm twice as much next year."

"I am going to get me one of those Wheatland Fordsons. This year I had in 160 acres of wheat and that made twenty bushels to the acre. If I had one of them big Wheatland tractors, I could farm three or four times as much."

The manager of the trading company spoke up and said, "You better settle up here before you go out and buy a tractor." They all got up and went home.

Next day I see salesmen by the dozens working the country. These farmers have made so much money this year that they will buy nearly anything. To name a few: sewing machines, washing machines, cream separators, wagons, buggies, cars, tractors. One guy is doing very good as a carbide light salesman. Some of the original homesteaders are ready to sell out due to health and not being able to farm anymore. Some of them have gotten too old, too. There has been a consolidation of farms. During the past ten years, about one-third of the homesteaders have moved away and a few more are leaving now that there is money to buy them out.

All the debts have been paid and the land is being prepared for next year.

The people are a happy bunch and have a dream of the future that crops will be good and they can improve their homesteads with good houses and outbuildings.

Most of the one-room schoolhouses have church on Sunday, with a minister coming about once a month from the big church in town. They have parties and dances in the schoolhouses on Saturday nights and everyone has a good time.

Each Saturday every farmer in the valley and mesa goes into town. They take their eggs and cream to sell if they have any extra. Even if they don't have anything to sell, they go to visit and talk farming.

I hear some big arguments going on. One farmer says, "I wouldn't live out there on the mesa and haul water for anything."

The farmer from the south says, "I know. Every time I get ready to move back east I can't go because I have to go haul water. I guess I am stuck out there. But I tell you what, I wouldn't farm those blue weeds out north for all the water in the world."

"That fellow over east of me bought a Poppin Johnnie and you can hear him from daylight to dark plowing with that thing. Now, I have Alice Chalmer, that is the tractor, but I tell you one thing, you better watch that cultivator; it will cut your fingers off if you get them in the wrong place."

"That A.C. may be okay, but I like the Farmall better, especially if you cut the wheels down and put them on rubber tires. I believe I can do more work on less gas than any other tractor."

They go on and on until nearly sundown. The young people have found out where the dance is going to be that night and the housewife has bought the week's grocery supply. They stop by the filling station on the way out and fill up so they will have enough to get back to town next Saturday. The tractors burn purple gas and they dare not use it in the car or truck, as it is against the law. There is a tax refund on tractor gas.

Maybe I should explain to you a little more about the land and what is happening to it. Now, in this valley the wind blows nearly every March and a few days in the fall, especially since the land has been put into farms. The way they farm beans, they don't leave any mulch or cover on the ground. Therefore, with the least stirring of the wind, the sand kicks up and the topsoil moves to the east. It will bank up on the fencerows where the tumbleweeds are captured and sometimes block the road. Now that the farmers have tractors, they have learned that if they will plow the land in the fall after the crops are in, it will not blow so hard. The way the plowing is done with a tractor is to plow every other furrow with a moleboard plow as deep as they can pull, then go back in the spring and plow the furrow they had skipped. When using teams, they usually plow two rows and skip two. That way they can contain the land in both the fall and spring. Now, the next few years after the big crops are just mediocre and the people are just barely able to hold their own, living in hopes of next year. This is the time of the depression and dust bowl back seat. Bean prices went to rock bottom and it was hard to find anyone to buy them. Surely next year will be better.

It would be twelve years before another crop.

It is a shame what happens to the valley during this time. I somehow feel that the valley is part of me and anything that hurts it hurts me. As I watch, a half-section just over two miles north of Mountainair and on the west side of the road just breaks my heart. Nearly all of it has been in cultivation for over twenty years and now that there is no rain there is just no way to keep it from blowing. These last few years the wind starts just after sunup and blows hard every day. It appears that as the sand picks up, the wind velocity also increases—therefore, a vicious circle. Very often I am not able to see the ground out there for the amount of sand in the air. The half- section that I spoke of has lost all of its topsoil and is down to caliche all over. It is just like an open sore. All over the valley it is nearly as bad as it was when the lakes dried up. One poor guy brought in a bunch of sheep, thinking they could live on what little vegetation there was, but it wasn't long until they were blind from the sand and their wool was so heavy they just laid down and died.

The ground is so hard and dry that it is impossible to plow or do anything with it. More and more, I see farmers just load up their household possessions and leave out. No one wants to or has the money to buy them out. The sand piles up around the barns and houses. It gets inside the attics and brings the ceilings down. Some say that the sand will go through glass windows. Everyone goes around with a handkerchief over his face to keep the sand out of his lungs. All dishes on the table must be upside down and still when the food is served it tastes gritty. The housewives chink up all cracks around the windows and hang a quilt over the doors to try to keep it out. Several babies and older people suffocate from the amount of sand in the air. Livestock everywhere suffers and dies.

Most of the roads have sand banks that cannot be driven through. They just take the fence down and drive around them out in the field or pasture.

The wind and sand combination build up a static electricity that will cause a motor not to run. Some people have got caught out with a stalled engine and have to wait until sundown, when the wind dies down, before they can go on. "More people leave in the dark"—that is a saying they have for someone owing debts all over and slipping out without paying them.

I overheard a farmer from way down south that was going to plow four hundred acres of beans say, "I sold John W. a quarter-section of land but I really stuck it to him. I deeded him 320."

Several places over the valley are being sold for taxes.

Then the government steps in. (I wish I could talk to them, too.) They told the farmer, "You plant them beans out there and when they get blooms on them, you plow them under. Don't you know they are a legume and will fertilize that soil and you can double your yield next year? We will pay you to do that."

They also have a program called the rehab (rehabilitation). They would loan money to buy tractors and equipment and seed and everything it took to make a crop. Some of the farmers took advantage of it while others would have nothing to do with it as it smacked of welfare and these are a proud people.

I am going back to the fellow that traded his house for a team of little red mules and came home to his in-laws with the flu. He is the same fellow that traded one hundred sacks of beans for a new six-cylinder Chevrolet. Let's call him Mac. He managed by hard work and being lucky to purchase 320 acres out there before the wind started so bad. Bill White has a school section just across the section line and he makes a deal with Mac to farm that. He will furnish eight head of good work stock and all the seed and feed, and take one third of the crop for rent.

That makes Mac a total of eight hundred acres to farm. He planted all eight hundred acres and did not harvest a bean that year. Bill White went bankrupt and died shortly after that.

Mac harvested green tumbleweeds to feed his livestock and by working a few days on W.P.A. he was able to hang on to his land.

The next year is a lot better, but he is not farming so much land and he has purchased a tractor on payments. Now, on the 10th of May it comes twelve inches of snow. Mac has already planted ten acres, which he must plant over or the weeds will take it. On the 15th of September it comes twelve inches of snow. His beans are in the pile. The wind blows for two days and all that can be seen are mounds of sand. He is able to dig some of them out with a fork. He gets enough beans to make his payments and pay the grocery bill at the trading company.

Mac goes back to the rock crusher and works, leaving two of his six boys to farm. This year it has been twelve years since the last big crop and it doesn't look much better than a lot of other years. The boys get about four hundred acres planted with two Farmall regular tractors. It rains every Saturday just as regular as clockwork. Mac is working at the rock crusher and does not realize what is happening and the boys are too dumb to know until they start thrashing. Beans roll out of that spout faster than two men can take of them. Mac buys a new tractor. The boys go off to the army and the land once again starts to blow away. Mac wears out that new tractor the next few years trying to keep the land from blowing.

That is the last good crop to be raised in this valley. All sorts of things are tried. One fellow said, "Boy, I have found the answer—Sunflowers." Two years and weevils got in them so bad there was no market.

The government told the farmers the only thing to do is get some milk cows and sell milk. Now, an old black-and-white cow just can't produce milk eating sand. And that is about all there is left for them to eat.

Over 90 percent of the farmers have gone now. The land is bare, with no one to care for it. The wind blows day after day and the fences get covered and the roads blocked. Where someone has taken the government up and gone into the dairy business is a pitiful sight—trying to keep the sand out of the milk and buying every bit of feed. It is hard.

The wind blows and the boys come home from the war to abandoned places. Sand piled up over the tractor and equipment they left when they went off. Can't even get the barn door open. Most of them turned away with a tear in their eye and found a job working for wages. I heard several of these boys says, "If I could make a living out there farming beans, that is where I would be."

Again the valley is desolate, without very many people living out there. The sand blows every day. One place that is especially bad is west of Estancia. From the mountains to the salt lakes there is a strip about a mile wide that sand blows every day from sunup till sundown. The sand is covering houses, barns, and fences. Even land that has been used for pasture and never been plowed is blowing away.

The bean elevators in Mountainair are all closed and are being dismantled. The stores, the schools, and all the saloons except one are closed in Willard. It is nearly a ghost town. Estancia has one grocery store and one bean elevator. All country schools have been consolidated into the schools in Estancia, Mountainair, and Moriarty.

The Central New Mexico Railroad has gone broke and sold out to the Santa Fe now. They are taking up the rails and all that is left is a scar across the valley from north to south.

The government comes forth with another program that is called the soil bank. The way it works is if the farmer will lease his land to the government, seed it back to grass, and keep all livestock off it for ten years, the government will pay the farmers six dollars per acre per year. The farmer had only been able on an average to get three sacks at three cents, making nine dollars per acre with all of his work. Therefore, ninety-eight percent of the farmland is signed up and seeded back to grass. The wind and sand continues to blow and there is not enough moisture to start the grass.

Irrigation water has been discovered in the lower part of the valley, just west of the salt lakes. It appears to be an area about four miles wide east to west and extends from Willard on the south to north of Moriarty (it used to be called Buford). Some of the dryland bean farmers that had a little money left have purchased and developed farms there. Some are building nice homes and doing good. They are finding that a lot of different crops will grow here. They have planted beans, wheat, corn, barley, potatoes, carrots, pumpkins, squash, and alfalfa. The best operation seems to be a farm-livestock set up. Market is a problem for the garden-type producer. Beans are too expensive and hazardous to raise.

The dry land has long since come out of the soil bank and out there where there was a house on every quarter-section no one lives now. The land has been sold and blocked up into small ranches. The last of the original homesteaders have either passed on or moved away. After thirty years, the grass is growing back and the wind does not blow as it did before.

The scars are still on the land, to be seen by those that know what to look for, but the valley is still there in the summer of 1988.

Note

1. These must have resembled the jacals of their ancient predecessors in the times of Gran Quivira I.

6

The Book of Days: Vital Records from Gran Quivira

Introduction by the Authors

Almost fifty years ago, Dr. Merle Curti, our revered professor at Columbia University and the late emeritus professor of history at the University of Wisconsin, suggested that local newspapers were an important source for social history. Even though the quantity of newspaper sources was limited for this study, we felt personally that the people and events we learned about in our interviews were extended by reading the newspapers available in the University of New Mexico and the state archives in Santa Fe.

The people, the church, the school, the singing conventions, the "ruins," and the weather became more vividly alive to us. We would anticipate the next issue to see whether the storm or heat wave had subsided, the price of beans gone up or down and what social activities occurred. Actually, we wished we might have given this source more time, to present an even better vista view of this time and place.

Read the "Book of Days" before you examine the moldering fractionated foundation of the once-busy Main Street of Gran Quivira III. It could change your view of history and be a genuine historical experience for you.

The Dow family. Top: Ida, bottom: Elisha Jr., center row (from left to right): Daniel, Elisha Sr., Clara, and Barbarita.

1885 **Elisha A. Dow Diary, Notes**
—Had trouble with church and priest over firing of a teacher. I gave priest a hauling over about school matters.
—Pelts and wool are often my cargo.
—Often out hunting cattle. Lost some—found some unbranded.
—Went to meeting Sunday, August 2, 1885, to hear the Protestant tell falsehoods. We answered him in the evening.
—Bartoli Gonzalez, Viterli Luhan, and Antonio Chavez working together on water projects and prospecting for water.
—December 26, 1885—Barbarita Dow sick with rheumatism.[1] Doctor stayed several hours.
—Wolves bad all around.

1886 **E.A.D. Diary, Notes**
—Daniel Milton Dow born at home, October 30.
—Big seller was barbed wire for fencing.
—Had roundup at Stinking Springs.[2]
—Got hurt by bullfight.
—Spent time at home reading, when not a peddler.
—Gunfire broke doors and windows at Dow house at Gran Quivira. Guns fired by T. G. Duke and Daniel Sanchez. Sanchez shot in leg running away. Duke tried and found guilty. I was fined $25 plus costs. Arrested for protecting my property.

1887 **Dow found guilty and McAfee, also.**

1888 **E.A.D. Diary, Notes**
—Began reading Bible through.
—Spent about five days on a visit in Santa Fe. Saw many antelope.
—Did surveying for ranchers.

1889: Letter

Office of E. A. Dow
Dealer in
General Merchandise, Wool, Cattle Hides,
Pelts and All Kind of Country Produce
Post Office Address
Taique, (sic) N.M.

Taique, [sic] New Mexico
July 2, 1889

To His Excellency
Governor L. Bradford Prince,*
Santa Fe, N.M.
Dear Sir,

I take the liberty to write you a few lines concerning political affairs. If the President of the United States continues to ignor [sic] in his appointments our native citizens altogether the result in the coming compagne [sic] is very doubtful for our adversaries will work hard on that point. I have heard many thus express themselves not only about here but in Santa Fee [sic] & elsewhere. True some says there has only 3 applied & two of them their are serious charges against them. But let us incorrage [sic] others to apply for some office & do our best to get them appointed. It is a notorious fact that the democrat party did not ignor the Native citizens nor the Catholic Schools (indians) [sic] hoping you will excuse me for these few lines and suggestions.

I remain your friend,
E. A. Dow

*Prince, L. (LeBaron) Bradford 1840–1922—Conservative Republican from Flushing, New York. Appointed governor of New Mexico by President Harrison and served 1889 to 1893.

1891: Letter
Taique, N.M.
12-21-1891
Governor, L, Bradford prince [sic]
Dear Sir,
Your favor of 8th inst. received. Contents noted and my answer is yes I will accept the office of post master here at Taique.
Very truly yours,
E. A. Dow
P.S. I received this day notice and [illegible] concerning PO from PO Department which answered this date.

1895	**Author's Notes**

—Village of Gran Quivira, generally speaking, was constructed by rocks from the "ruins." A large beam over the doorway was pulled out and placed near Elisha Dow's first rock home down the hill in an area which was to become Gran Quivira village. Lintels and rocks disappeared as the town grew. Sizeable white limestone rocks were indigenous. The beams, requiring at least four men to move, came from the forests of the Gallinas Mountains, fifteen miles eastward.

1908	**Newspaper**

—*Mountainair News*

Letter from Rev. Thurston Brown (published by request) *Socialism,* Rochester, N.Y., 1908.

1909	**September 24, *Mountainair News***

Fraternal organizations in places like Gran Quivira:
AF and AM
Knights of Pythias
Rebecca Lodge
Workman of the World
Churches: Baptist, Methodist, Presbyterian, Catholic, Church of Christ, Pentecostal Holiness, Church of Nazarene.

1910 *Willard Record,* **Notes**[3]
—WCTU and Anti-Saloon League are advertising.
—Front page is more than half Spanish at times.
—Talk of the 8-hour day is round.
—Mr. Snyder, Socialist, spoke at the Tabernacle (Willard, NM) May 5th and again tonight on the Constitution.
—Mr. Gaurst got a nice bill of groceries from Sears Roebuck last week.

1916 **December 14,** *Willard Record*
—Roland Harwell, county agent: "a fairly accurate knowledge of the climatic conditions here, a good understanding of the principles of agriculture without irrigation and a vigorous application of these principles adapted to this climate will make dry farming failures a rarity."
—Front page more than half Spanish.
—Ten emigrant wagons arrived last week (Willard, October 16th).

1917 **November 8, 1917,** *Mountainair Independent*
—U.S. Army will pay seven and three fourths cent (sic) for Colorado and New Mexico pinto beans. State Food Administrator Ely received telegram from Food Administration in Washington.
—(Editorial) Labor unions are getting too strong. They are as ruthless as German Military Autocracy.

November 25–27, *Willard Record,* **Notes**
—Aldo Leopold spoke at State Teachers Convention on Wild Life Conservation.
—Baseball played in valley. The column in the paper entitled "Diamond Notes."

—Horse and foot races also popular. Fifty of the young men failed for the draft because of poor health.
—Literary societies well attended.

1917
—Catholic Church notices are beginning to appear.
—Frank Dow arrived from Flagstaff, Arizona, where he has been working in the mines.[4]

1918 **January 3, 1918,** *Willard Record*
Elisha Dow left Sunday afternoon for Flagstaff, Arizona, where he has secured employment in the mines. Dow attended the Fiesta at Chilili before he left.

March 26, 1918, *Mountainair Independent*
—Seven trainloads of soldiers passed through Mountainair on Monday of this week.

July (?) *Willard Record* **(Gran Quivira section)**
—A Fourth of July Fiesta given by William Randolph Hearst. His publications condemned by State Councils of Defense. He did not favor involvement of U.S. in World War I.

August 15, 1918, *Willard Record,* **Notes**
AN OUTRAGE TO NEW MEXICANS
An article in *North American Review* by Henry Wray, "Mexicans Are Traitors to the Government." Article defends New Mexicans and points out they have done well in Liberty Bonds purchases, Red Cross work, and Salvation Army drives.

1918 **September 26, 1918,** *Mountainair Independent, Liberty News (column)*[5]
—Mrs. W. D. Garrison not at all well.
—Farmers are harvesting hay and corn.

—Company is being organized to drill a well near Mr. Conders. The property belongs to the company. Mr. Whitlow is doing the work.

September 26, 1918, *Mountainair Independent*
—Ben Adams of Little Rock, Arkansas brought Sister Maggie to Liberty to visit brother Thomas Adams. Maggie will teach in Gran Quivira School. Likes it so well she put in a claim for 160 acres.

September 26, October 3, October 14, 1918, *Mountainair Independent*, Notes, "Personal and Local Items"
—Regular Preaching Dates
At Gran Quivira school house the 2nd Sunday at 11 A.M.
At Round Top the 3rd Sunday at 11 A.M. and at night.
      —W. D. Harrison, Pastor
—Quarantine for flu epidemic is in force.

November 14, 1918, *Willard Record*
—Big notice by the Surgeon General, Rupert Blue
SPANISH FLU EPIDEMIC IN TORRANCE COUNTY
—*Gran Quivira News* (column)
Snowdrifts 3 feet deep. No mail delivery. Joe Reid took a load of beans to Mountainair this week. W. D. Harrison sold mares to Thomas Adam. He lost a good horse, is the third to be lost in the past three years.

1918   **November 24, 1918, *Willard Record***
—The socialist candidate ran a good race (Eugene V. Debs) with other two parties.

December 12, 1918, *Willard Record*, News from Gran Quivira
—Spanish Flu an epidemic in Torrance County.

—Men called for examination for draft. Five from Quarai, one from Abo, none from Gran Quivira.

—Beans: Army Buys Beans (Headline p. 3)

—Jones Turner, Louise Kite's father, homesteaded in the Gran Quivira area in 1918. He farmed, took produce to Mountainair to sell. He used a buckwagon and burros. The trip usually took two days and he would camp all night at Comfort's Corner, about ten miles from Mountainair. Produce consisted of cantaloupe, watermelon, pinto beans, corn, potatoes, pumpkins, and squash.

1919

January 9, 1919, *Mountainair Independent*

—The school at Centerpoint, first known as Anglin School, moved to Gran Quivira.

—Considering the weather and the fact nothing was certain about having service, the Sunday school and preaching service was well attended at Gran Quivira School House. The Pastor's subject was "Home, Heaven, and Hell." Let us all come out and help in the work.

—W. D. Harrison

—J. W. Garrison and J. M. Reed went to Belen Saturday night in search of work as the weather is so they can do nothing on their bean farms.

February 20, 1919, *Mountainair Independent*

—A Centerpoint petition was sent to county commissioners for a new precinct in this vicinity to save voters from long trips to the polls.

—Centerpoint reported W. D. Whitlow, W. D. Garrison, and William Edwards went to Estancia about the new precinct to be named Wilson, and Liberty School House the seat.

February 26, 1919, *Mountainair Independent*

—"The singing at J. W. Garrison's Sunday night was attended by such a crowd that the sleepers [beams on which wheel house rested] of the house broke, letting the floor down, but the organ was propped up and singing went on and such good singing. Oh my! It was enjoyed by all."[6]

May 8, 1919, *Mountainair Independent*
—The play "Money Bags" at Gran Quivira school house was good. Lum Fulfer represented "Money Bags."

May 18, 1919, *Mountainair Independent*
—Rev. J. Whitlow's son in France brought home a French girl to marry.

June 19, 1919, *Mountainair Independent,* **Friction**
—Centerpoint: "Some men from 60 to 70 miles south of here traced a horse thief to a little south of here and recovered two horses and a mule. They found a man riding one of their animals and took their stock."

July 3, 1919, *Mountainair Independent*
—Fourth of July picnic at Centerpoint. Free lemonade, foot races, horse races, girl races, Bronco riding, Kaiser and Devil fight.

July 31, 1919, *Mountainair Independent*
—Centerpoint: "The Union Protracted meeting will commence night before the second Sunday in August at the Gran Quivira schoolhouse and will continue for ten days or two weeks. All are invited to come and help. Rev. W. D. Garrison and Rev. J. S. Whitlow will be pastors in charge."

August 21, 1919, *Mountainair Independent*
—Mr. J. W. Garrison has purchased a Ford. Now, remember, it is Mr. Garrison.

September 4, 1919, *Mountainair Independent*
—Twenty four notices publicizing available lands appear in the Homestead section.

September 11, 1919, *Mountainair Independent*
—Thirty one notices applying (filing for homestead).

September 18, 1919, *Mountainair Independent*
—R. C. Beatty brought the Independent Family a half dozen fine specimens of Honey Dew melons grown on his farm near Gran Quivira. He also has a fine lot of watermelons.

October 16, 1919, *Mountainair Independent*
—Quite a few patrons met on Monday afternoon and hauled wood for the school. We are furnishing wood and water gratis to pay the teacher full price allowed per room.

November 13, 1919, *Mountainair Independent*
—From an article published in the *El Paso Herald* November 12: "Many new farmers have come into this section this season and also a number of new people for the town. Gran Quivira, the famous Spanish ruin, is being rapidly taken up by homesteaders."

1923

—Jack Kite rescued the Visitor Registration Book from the junk heap when attendants were moving the museum. Every page is of great interest. People walked to visit the monument, came by horses and cars. (Fords were most usual)

—Mr. and Mrs. Jones Turner shoveled to town Saturday. All who went along had plenty of exercise.

—Marshal Orme's column: "When spring comes, if it

ever does, the last man we want to see in town is a bean farmer."

1934 August, 1934, *Mountainair Independent*
—Revivals held in schools were sometimes called "singing societies."

—Dramas produced were religious in nature with titles like: "Disobedience to God" and "The Lonesome Bibles." Leaders in the sings and other religious conversations and revivals were called "Christ's ambassadors."

July 26, 1934, *Mountainair Independent*
—Prices for beans ain't going to start going up until they get higher than they are today.

September 7, 1934, *Mountainair Independent, (Headline)*

BEANS RISE $2.00 PER HUNDRED IN A WEEK'S TIME. NOW $5.00 PER HUNDRED

October 5th
—Threshing not in full steam.

1935 April—Southwestern Monuments, Superintendent's Monthly Reports
—Custodian for Gran Quivira ruins was George Boundey, who reported 281 visitors in July, 729 in August. Principal crop still beans: "Getting bumper crops." In recent years crop has been cut in half by no rain. Lots of rattlers in the "ruins." Hide and keep cool in the rocks. First talk of need for a new museum. Texans came searching for treasures. Robbery at ruins February 11th. Sheriff of Socorro investigated. Reported done "by men who knew the roads in area, knew the lay

of the lands and back roads."[7] Highway 14 (55) was developed by the WPA. The Anglos preferred calling the area "The Grand Quivira Monument." Gold seekers not happy when the government says any treasure discovered belongs to it, because "We know where to look!" One visitor came to dig. He took a nickel and put it in his palm, then wound fishnet line in some special way, back and forth until the "instrument" sagged on one said. There would be the lucky spot. "No," said Doc Smith, custodian, "you are over a kiva."

—A sewer and a septic tank have been installed at the "ruins."

—Doc William H. Smith walked uphill to the ruins to "check them over" every day when he was custodian and received 50¢ a day, five days a week. [Interview with Jack Kite in 1991.]

—"One reason for the unusual registration of the month was the county singing convention held at Gran Quivira on June 23, 1935. On that day I registered 520 persons. That is the one and only time that I could not give a little of my undivided attention. But they were just coming so fast that day that I did well to keep them registered.

"I got two of my boys to help me watch and see that things were orderly, and to give the very best service possible considering we were so crowded for time.

"On July 14, Reverend Huff, of Lovington, New Mexico, came here on his way to Corona, N.M., to a singing convention. Mr. Huff, having quite a congregation with him, assembled his party in the Mission and preached to them. Afterward they went on to Corona where the Huff sisters gave a recital. They are a famous quartet who sing quite often for broadcasting."—Superintendent's Report, p. 9.

—Supt. Boundey Reporting: "This country is so overgrazed by cattle and sheep, our monument is like an oasis in a desert when it comes to wild flowers. At night the air is so fragrant from the many *varieties of blossoms* one almost hates to waste his time in sleep."

1936 *Mountainair Independent,* **Notes from the column of J. C. Fulfer, correspondent for Gran Quivira**
—Ten thousand bags of beans a day have been cleaned in Mountainair. Five plants are in operation.
—"Many singing conventions were held at Centerpoint [a settlement four miles northwest of Gran Quivera] with overflowing attendance." Free lunch of "fryed [sic] chicken and other delicacies." Elected officers including a chaplain.
—Clyde Kite of Chaunok opened his home for a "nicetime" party, where dancing went on.
—Visitors at the local church on Sunday came over to the "ruins" to picnic after services. A space was set aside for them on the west side, beyond the pump house. Here they may build fires and pitch tents. This prevents children racing around on the walls.
—Dust was a growing problem![8] High winds blew sand and dust over the green bean plants, causing an almost complete crop failure.
—Infestation of goats running loose to ruin bean crop and trample the mission walls still standing. Joe Toulouse, Jr. came on as custodian of the ancient walls.

Mountainair Independent, **October 20, 1936**
—Educational pictures were shown Tuesday night at the WPA (Works Project Administration) School. The first reel was on Indian pottery. The different tribal patterns were contrasted. The second reel took spectators on an imaginary trip through the different forests in the United States.
—The WPA School is one of the interesting projects in the community. Many of the people are taking hold and making use of this opportunity in making better homes. The nurse class on Tuesday afternoon is being conducted by Hazel Lassereff, of matters to mothers and

wives. The nurse examined the children's eyes at the WPA School.

—Mrs. Beulah Claunch went to Estancia Friday on business in connection with the WPA School.

—Republicans held a meeting at High School Wednesday night. They held a Box Supper for the benefit of the School.

Mountainair Independent, **November 21, 1936**

—Complete returns for Torrance County—about 60 persons voted 2 to 1 Democrat.

Gran Quivira voted in Primary Election. The Democrat vote was Senator 19, Governor 21, State Auditor 19, State Senator 21, County Commissioner 1st Dist. 17, 2nd Dist. 20, 3rd Dist. 29—Probate Judge 19. The Republican vote for most offices was 2—a few offices had only 1 vote.

Mountainair Independent, **November 21, 1936**

—Hunting season is over. Gran Quivira hunters were very lucky. Almost every boy brought home a deer. Now the question has arisen causing considerable argument, "Which is better eating, the buck or the doe?"

Mountainair Independent, **December 10, 1936**

—All Gran Quivira should be extra sweet this Christmas. Jones Turner of Gran Quivira Mercantile Co. has over 600 pounds of Christmas candy.

—Representatives of the Telephone Company in Albuquerque were here taking pictures. We would love to have a nice telephone here.

—Poor attendance at church the last two Sundays. Brother Wells will be glad to meet all the old and also new faces in church Sunday.

Mountainair Independent, **December 17, 1936**

—Gran Quivira is having a boom. Four new buildings have been erected in the last thirty days.

—Gran Quivira school is having its program [Christmas].[9] Teachers have worked hard to make it a success.

1937 *Mountainair Independent,* **January 7, 1937**
—The Harrisons gave a dance New Year's night in honor of their son who has just returned from Texas.
—Jones Turner has electric lights in his store. Also a beautiful Christmas tree with electric lights.
—The Wake held at the Church, New Year's Eve, was well attended.

Mountainair Independent, **October 12, 1937**
—The annual Bean Festival was held October 12. It started with the Yellowstone Carnival. Beans and coffee were served at noon—200 pounds of beans and 40 pounds of Magnolia Coffee. There were special races; foot races, sock races, fat women's race. In the evening there were three kinds of dances—square dances for the older folks, swing dances with Al Stoval's orchestra for the younger ones and a Spanish dance for the Spanish people.

1938 *Mountainair Independent,* **November 11**
—Dennis Chavez not too popular in Gran Quivira. "This town has always been a nest of Democrats where a Republican was forced to have a passport before entering, but they are wondering now just why they are forgotten by everyone but the tax collector, and will no doubt express their distaste at polling time," J. C. Fulfer. "They should consider the Townsend Plan and run a new ticket."

1939 *Mountainair Independent,* **January 12, 1939, headline, front page**
BEAN SECTION HAS HEAVIEST SNOW IN 20 YEARS
Gran Quivira Column
Gran Quivira decided to stay home Monday or rather the weather man sent enough snow to keep us home a day. The Opportunity Club met last Thursday and completed a very pretty quilt. All report a very fine time.
—(Marshal Orme writes a column for this newspaper—"Here and There.") "One thing we can say for Tingley, he did not put his wife on the payroll." Orme

complained about government public employees putting family members on payroll.

1939 *Mountainair Independent,* **January 19**

—Roads to Gran Quivira and Claunch are bad. Rowena Yarborough spent the entire day going from Gran Quivira to Mountainair. The snow was drifted badly. The party expects to spend the night in Mountainair and return Thursday.

Mountainair Independent, **February 2**

—We really thank the road grader for removing the snow out of the road so we can see the wrinkles in the road. Rough spots aren't as bad as the snow.

Mountainair Independent **February 16**

—Bean Week a decided success. Beans prepared at State Penitentiary.

Mountainair Independent, **February 23**

—The fair city of Gran Quivira can boast of one electric light in the home of Mr. and Mrs. Idzar.

Mountainair Independent, **editorial, March 2**

UTILITIES STILL RULE NEW MEXICO

The fourteen legislature is keeping New Mexico legislative record clean in its dealing with the utilities. The present legislature is highly utility minded. It has killed the bill designed to regulate the utilities and now has passed a wage and hour law but it exempts women and girls employed in telephone and telegraph companies. They want the privilege of working girls in New Mexico as long as possible. This is somewhat after the fashion of the manufacturers and sweatshops in New England. In fact, the policies of the utilities in New Mexico are now dictated by Wall Street. And the various legislatures of New Mexico since statehood see fit that the utilities run the State in any manner they see fit and expedient. The exemption of girls from these corporations is another example of "Special privilege legislation all too prevalent in the United States.

One of the reasons the majority of the business interests of the nation are against Roosevelt is the fact he will not continue to rob the people through "special privilege" laws. New Mexico does lip service to the New Deal and then takes one of the most backward steps of any state in the Union.

Mountainair Independent, March 2

—Completion of Highway 60 should be a major issue. It would provide one link to the shortest transcontinental route. Those who want it completed as soon as possible should sign a petition to Governor Miles to make it one of his major projects 1939–40.

Mountainair Independent editorial, March 9

—A drive in any direction from Mountainair discloses another waste of natural resources all too common in the West. Farms have been allowed to blow until in many cases the soil is entirely gone and nothing remains but rock and packed earth. In practically ninety percent of these cases the farms in the worst shape are those that have been rented from year to year. The owner-farmer should make efforts to conserve his soil and improve it if possible. The itinerant renter has no interest in the land other than the present year. He looks neither to the past or the future. Absentee ownership of land ruined New England as a farming district. It has brought to the South the use of expensive fertilizers and bids fair to Torrance County to produce another dust bowl. And we still continue to clear more land so we plow it and let it blow away and produce more beans to add to an already overstocked market. The old familiar answer is, there ought to be a law. Yes, there ought to be a law. But more needed than a law are citizens who are builders and not despoilers and exploiters.

Mountainair Independent, April 6, Gran Quivira note

—The Fellowship Meeting held here Friday and Saturday was well attended. Rev. Bates of Clovis and Rev. Jackson of Albuquerque presided at the meeting. Folks came from Clovis, Corona, Carrizozo, Belen, Socorro and Mountainair.

***Mountainair Independent,* April 22**
—An Adult School opened at Gran Quivira with day and evening classes. Has been well attended. Music, English, History, and Arithmetic have been offered. Teachers are Mrs. L. H. Claunch and Bessie Means. Visiting nurse in county is very busy, especially with children.
—G. C. "Lum" Fulfer was killed when horses pulling his wagon ran away, four miles from Gran Quivira. He was buried at White Lakes Cemetery.
—Roy Montgomery and Stennie Russell in charge of "the big two-day rodeo." Admission will be 35 cents and includes the baseball game.
—Many Assembly of God camp meetings go on at Gran Quivira with "eats and shelter provided."
—A Baptist minister in the area was Lorenzo Dow Sanders.[10] There is talk among the bean farmers of organizing Cooperative Marketing to protect prices paid to farmers.

***Mountainair Independent,* April 27, advertisement**
—Subscribe to the *Christian Science Monitor*

***Mountainair Independent,* June 15, Centerpoint news**
—Mrs. And Mrs. V. O. Wells entertained a few friends at an outdoor supper Saturday evening. Those present were J. N. Underwood and daughters, Mr. and Mrs. Bure Tate, Mr. and Mrs. Skid Wells and babies, Art Garrison, Mr. and Mrs. Engles Tomlinson and son, Mr. and Mrs. Homer Lewis and A. A. Wood. All reported a nice time with plenty to eat and drink.

***Mountainair Independent,* June 27**
—Gran Quivira must be living right. We are getting some very good rain.
—Almost all of Gran Quivira attended the picnic at Claunch last Wednesday and had a very nice time.

Mountainair Independent, **July 20**
—Little Jackie Kite was quite ill last week but is much better now.

—A group of people of Gran Quivira enjoyed a fishing trip to San Marcia three days last week. They reported a very nice time and an abundance of fish. They were Mr. and Mrs. Jones Turner, Elsie and Julia Mae, Mr. and Mrs. Alton Thornton, his mother and brother Rex; Mr and Mrs. Truman Thornton and Viola; Mr. and Mrs. Diering, Sonny and Cynthia.

1939 *Superintendent's Monthly Report,* **August**
—Road from Mountainair to Gran Quivira is going to be improved. Trying to cap and gravel it by WPA will improve attendance. 545 visitors, 134 vehicles.

—W. H. "Doc" Smith took great care of the ruins. Fixed the roof himself. "I think now it will be safe." (p. 94)

Mountainair Independent, **August 10**
—Pat Shaw is the new custodian at Gran Quivira. We certainly are glad to have him and his mother in our community.

—Gov. (John E. Miles) gave a banquet for Pop Shaffer but could not attend because of illness. It was a decided success. After the banquet the Chamber of Commerce took the guests to the ruins at Abo and Quari.[11] (By this time some feeling was developing that Gran Quivira should remain independent of Abo and Quari.) (BML)

Mountainair Independent, **August 17**
—Singing convention to meet in Claunch, Sunday, August 27. Shortage of funds, so paper cups and paper plates will not be furnished.

—Wedding in Gran Quivira. Lillian Jones, raised near Gran Quivira, married Mr. Albert Edge of Mountainair in his parents' home. Rev. H. M. Fulfer read the ring ceremony.

Mountainair Independent, **August 31, Headline**
QUIVIRA ROAD SHOULD BE REPAIRED
Highway to Gran Quivira has been washed out a month.

No state agency or any government body has made repairs. Highway is a state road, a route to Gran Quivira. It serves large portions of Mountainair trade area. State and national officials have been notified. Can't be politics because this area is predominantly Democratic. "What is the trouble?" A few dollars and a few men are needed. What is the matter and who is responsible?

—Voters Registration Listed

Democrats 2,657, Republicans 1,983—difference 674. Gran Quivira—6 Republicans, 27 Democrats (decline of 20). "In the last election 631 voted in both divisions of Mountainair. Wilson showed strongly Democratic as did Gran Quivira, Lacers, and Cedarvale."

Mountainair Independent, **October 24**

—Front Page of *Mountainair Independent* for this issue had an article, "Gran Quivira Road in Bad Condition." Need to improve to harvest bean crop. Repair also affects the Mesa country and Mountainair.

Mountainair Independent, **October 27**

—Almost everyone in Gran Quivira went to Claunch to the singing convention on Sunday. Everyone reported a wonderful time and a delicious dinner.

—Revival at Assembly of God church started Monday night. Brother Babson of Albuquerque in church each evening this week.

Mountainair Independent, **November 2**

—Proposed tariff reduction hurt local bean industry. Governor Miles is opposed.

—November 9, 1939, Mountainair Townsend Club was organized. Six people came to the meeting.

1940 *Mountainair Independent,* **passim**

—Gran Quivira was a Precinct in 1940–50.

Population in 1940 in Precinct 26: 113

Population in 1950 in Precinct 26: 78

(Precinct disappeared after 1950.)

—A bean surplus in May 1940. Beans given to the Red Cross.

—Election results at September 14 Primary at Gran Quivira.
  2 Republicans
  11 Dennis Chavez, Democrat
  8 Dempsey, Democrat
—General Election, November 1940
  17 Republicans in village at Abo
  106 Democrats in Abo
  30 Democrats in Gran Quivira
—The government is buying beans!
—Doc Smith has moved to Alamagordo. One of the important figures in Gran Quivira history.
—As bean cropping begins to fail, many are moving to California, some back East to former homes.

***Mountainair Independent,* 1940, passim**
—Travelers to the Gran Quivira Monument were of interest to the local citizens. The caretakers have usually lived in the village and they and their families participated in the community activities, like church and school. Travelers came to buy food, gasoline, and have minor repairs for the car and just to "visit" in the village. Local papers gave statistics of the yearly number of visitors and cars with state licenses and the make of the car.

***The Mountainair Independent* c. 1940**
—The *Independent* reveals activities of an organization for women which was active for many years, called the Opportunity Club. According to one newspaper account, it began in October 13, 1938—open to all women in the community. The club met on Thursday. Sometimes there were pot luck affairs and at times members brought their own sandwiches. At first they seem to have met in the building owned by the mattress company before it faded away in Gran Quivira. The women cleaned the building and took care of surrounding trees and flowers. A chief project was making an applique quilt top for every member and one for the

club. Handkerchief showers were given to honor birthdays. The newspaper records reveal that sometimes every member of the Opportunity Club was present or all the women of the community were present. Games were played and a croquet court was maintained in the yard.

—Visiting organizations for local, state, and even national meetings were encouraged to visit the ruins. President Taft is recorded to have visited in 1918. Local residents, as well as visitors, often had picnics in or near the ruins.

—Singing conventions, which were monthly, bimonthly, and often weekly occasions, were still the most famous "entertainments." However, the annual Bean Day must not be overlooked. It occurred after the bean harvest. Often it included the annual Boys and Girls Club fairs. Races, dominoes, cards, and croquet were played. The great event was the menu—baked beans, boiled beans, bean salad, beans and chili, stewed beans, and bean soup.

Mountainair Independent, **January 11, Gran Quivira**
—Wanda Garrison wed Clyde Jackson on January 5. Ceremony was in home of Anne Mell Austin, by Rev. Wells. James Connell was best man and Anne Mell Austin was maid of honor. Guests present were Nora Wells, Inez Austin, Edith Shaw, Myrtle Ola McNutt, Essie Jo Turner, Jeannette Garrison, Mrs. Wells, Mrs. Smith, Mr. and Mrs. Thorton, Rev. Wells, and the bride and groom. The couple left for trip to Santa Fe. They will make their home in Gran Quivira.

Mountainair Independent, **January 18, notice**
—To Whom It May Concern:
—If you are expecting the stork to visit your house this year, and he is to come by the way of Moutainair, he will have to bring cash to pay his bill before delivery, as the undersigned doctors delivered many babies during 1938 and 1939 and over half are not paid for.

We do not need the experience and if you cannot pay the bill, please do not call us, as we will not render services without payment in advance. Since you have had nine months to pay for this expense.

To those who have not paid for their 1938 and 1939 bill in full or made a satisfactory arrangement to do so, do like the stork—be sure to bring the money when you call again.

***Mountainair Independent*, January 25, lead editorial**
—Carlsbad editor complains that local communities are assessed for the Coronado Cuerto Centennial. Not surprised because Carlsbad has nothing to offer—nothing that has anything to do with Coronado. Coronado was fired by the fabulous treasure of Gran Quivira (25 mi. southeast of Mountainair). "Coronado was not interested in the rapid growth of Albuquerque nor its bank clearings. And Chaco Canyon and Santa Fe don't seem to be on his itinerary. But he was intensely interested in the Cities of Cibola. Mountainair is the heart and 'inspiration' of the present day interest in Coronado's magnificent gesture."

***Mountainair Independent*, February 22, lead editorial**
MOUNTAINAIR NEEDS MORE PUBLICITY
National magazines which advertise New Mexico do not give enough attention to Mountainair. Gran Quivira and Abo are reached through Mountainair but not even mentioned.

—County 4H Club has attendance of 150.

***Mountainair Independent*, May 30 passim**
—The Opportunity Club entertained a covered dish luncheon. It was a celebration of WPA School projects all over the country. Mrs. Dean Miller gave a talk on the advantages the school has for everyone. Mrs. Opal Fulfer was the president, Mrs. N. L. Anglin the secretary, and Mrs. L. Claunch was the treasurer.

—In Mountainair there are organizations that are open to

women in Gran Quivira, e.g. the Cow Belles, Eastern Star, and the Coronado Club.

—*Hunting and Fishing*

Whether one would label it sport or providing food—from the beginning, hunting during the autumn was a pastime or an economic necessity. Newspapers annually reported the bagging of deer as "good and bad luck." In the spring, men and boys ventured into hunting rattlesnakes. These were plentiful but no one reported eating them. Summers were given to fishing but it involved travel to lakes.

***Mountainair Independent,* April 18**

—At this time of the year all the boys went around to Claunch to go rattlesnake hunting. Some men enjoy the sport of killing the pests. "Mr. Jones and Desmond Winters killed [sic] 91 rattlesnakes Sunday. They caught them coming out of their dens and shot them in the head."[12]

***Mountainair Independent,* May 2, headline**

THE GRAN QUIVIRA OPPORTUNITY CLUB MEETS WITH MRS. BILL DYER

The Gran Quivira Opportunity Club met with Mrs. Bill Dyer in the Centerpoint Community, Thursday, April 25. A potluck lunch/dinner was served to the following members and guests: Mrs. Anglin, Mrs. Claunch, Mrs. Talbert, Mrs. Gennings, Rowena Yarborough, Mrs. C. B. Anderson, Mrs. C. C. Airheart, Bessie Gentry, Mrs. Hoss Whitehead, Mrs. Stevens, Mrs. Bishop, and the hostess, Mrs. Dyer.

A handkerchief shower was given Mrs. Young in honor of her birthday.

The day was spent in sewing and playing cards. Mrs. Stephens, Mrs. Bishop, and Mrs. Airheart entertained with a song.

***Mountainair Independent,* May 16**

—The Gran Quivira School will be completed this week.

—Beans are being planted at the rate of 400 acres per day. All parts of the county report plenty of moisture.

—Effort is being made to interest farmers in buying soy beans. The seed is not expensive, seeds fertilize the ground, and there is a cash market for soy beans.

Mountainair Independent, **May 30**

—Mr. and Mrs. J. Tulouse, custodian of Gran Quivira ruins, were Santa Fe visitors this week.

—Headline

OPPORTUNITY CLUB ENTERTAINS

Covered dish luncheon—over 100 people attended. It was a get together week of celebration all over the country by WPA School projects. Games were the chief entertainment.

Mountainair Independent, **June 6**

—Clerks for registration and voting were announced for Gran Quivira: (1) Mrs. Carl U. Jones; (2) Mrs. Dean Miller.[13]

Mountainair Independent, **June 19**

—The news notes in the Gran Quivira column has three items encouraging the planting of soy beans. It is suggested to buy them from J. W. Jackson.

Mountainair Independent, **June 20**

—Rotary sponsored a Goodwill picnic at Claunch. 400 persons came. Coffee and beans were supplied by Rotary.

—Claunch is building a town. Other places are losing. Enthusiasm is the difference.

Mountainair Independent, **July 4**

—Jimmy Wells and 13 Gran Quivirans attended the Assembly of God meeting in Albuquerque Friday.

—Jim Garrison and the surveyors were in Gran Quivira looking the electric light situation over.

Mountainair Independent, **July 11**

—The tourist season has really started. We have cars from almost every state coming to see the ruins. There was Fourth of July fishing on the Rio Grande.

Mountainair Independent, **July 29**
—L. H. Claunch has a celebration—birthday and wedding anniversary. Calves are rounded up and branded. Lives 10 miles south of Gran Quivira. (Mrs. Kite reported he always identified himself with Gran Quivira.)

Mountainair Independent, **August 1**
—The headline of the newspaper read: EFFORT BEING MADE TO DISPOSE OLD CROP PINTOS. Beans dropped to $2.50 a bushel. Torrance County has 75,000 bags of beans from 1939 to 1940 and the present crop is ready to be harvested. Local Red Cross and Surplus Commodity have been asked to purchase the beans and distribute them in Europe.

Mountainair Independent, **August 1**
—Assembly of God church is getting a coat of paint and general housecleaning to get ready for the big meeting on August 9th.

Mountainair Independent, **August 15, headline**
MEETINGS TO DISPOSE OF OLD BEANS ARE HELD BY FARMERS
One hundred farmers attended. 27,000 bags at $3.25 have to be cleaned at 50¢ a hundred.

Mountainair Independent, **August 22**
—CAMP MEETING—August 9–19, of the Assembly of God Church. 500 in attendance. Visitors from Arkansas and Arizona.

Mountainair Independent, **September 19**
—How Torrance County voted in Primary—Gran Quivira Democrats: senator 19, governor, 21, state auditor 19; county commission: 1st division 17, 2nd division 20 probate judge 19, representative 21. *Republicans:* senator 2, representative 2, governor 2, other offices 1 or 2 votes.

1941 **January 31, 1941—The *Mountainair Independent* to close. Last issue was April 25, 1941.**
—Gran Quivira—"Young People Club Meets Saturday Night" (Assembly of God group)

- —Assembly of God rallies gathered at Gran Quivira from Albuquerque—Belen, Grants, Mountainair.
- —Friday night Club reported large crowd.
- —Had a women's missionary society.
- —Every column devoted to Gran Quivira "Come to the Assembly of God in Gran Quivira."
- —90 attended church April 4, 1941. Some came over from Claunch to sing.
- —Draftees leaving for war.
- —L. H. Claunch always more active in Gran Quivira than with is church in Claunch, the village named for his family.

1943 *Mountainair Independent:* **This paper ceased to exist.**
- —Mary Jo Russell and Mrs. Charles Fulfer were the last Gran Quivira correspondents. H. C. Fulfer was a regular correspondent for this paper before it closed its doors. He wrote a column titled "I Was Just Thinking," filled with attractive satire and political comment about Gran Quivira. He supported the Townsend Movement, whose main goal was to have Congress pay all senior citizens an adequate retirement pension—money would trickle up rather than down (!), factories would get more orders for goods, and jobs would be increased by demands on capitalist producers, thus stopping the "Great Depression."

Mountainair Progressive **November 5, Mrs. John Montgomery, reporter**
- —"Looks like everyone in the country is leaving us. Mr. and Mrs. Ed Boggos and family are leaving for California by the first of the year and it is rumored we are also losing Johnnie Johnson. Wonder what the population of Gran Quivira is coming to ????"

November 12, Gran Quivira news by Mrs. John Montgomery
- —Mr. and Mrs. Jack Kite have moved into their new home.
- —Essie Joe Turner is to be married to a soldier in Lub-

bock Saturday night. Mr. and Mrs. Jones Turner, Mrs. Truman Thorton, and Mrs. Jack Kite have left to attend the wedding.

1943 *Mountainair Progressive,* **November 26**
—Centerpoint: Deer Season has come to a close at last. Lucky hunters are J. W. Harrison and son, Boyce, Rubin Garrison, and J. W. Anglin ten point buck.

Mountainair Progessive, **December 10**
—Lots of moving around in the country for the farmers: Lloyd McMath moved from the Jackson farm at Ewing. Roth McMath from the Ewing place to his father's farm, Bill McMath moved to Hot Springs, Roy McMath from south of town to the C. S. Messanger place, Abb Farmer from Lee Briggs place to Johnny Auferoths, and Chig Farmer to Briggs farm and Jimmy Jones moved on the Hoyland place. All hoping to make a good crop once more.

—J. W. Garrison had a big auction—successful. Large crowd attend from Gran Quivira, Mountainair, and Claunch. Mr. and Mrs. Garrison and three youngest children are going to a new home in Arkansas. Mrs. Garrison has been in the hospital.

1944 *Mountainair Progressive,* **January 7, 1944**
—Red Cross reports Torrance County fell far below its quota in war relief production.

—Torrance County, Consumer Cooperative, is holding an all-day meeting today in Estancia. Harvy Solberg, Rocky Mountain Union president, will be the main speaker. He has been to England recently, invited by the British minister of agriculture to study food, agriculture, and the cooperative system.

Mountainair Progressive, **January 21**
—Roads are in such bad shape no mail is delivered. Mr. and Mrs. John Montgomery were stranded in Mountainair from Monday to Thursday.

Centerpoint **news column**
—The big snowstorm of last Sunday, a week ago,

blocked travel over the highway until last Friday, when the mail was delivered for the first time in a week. The school bus has been unable to come for the children. Hope it can make the trip for this week as the back lessons will be hard to make up. Travel has been light this way, done either by tractor, horseback, or on foot.

1944 *Mountainair Progressive,* **January 21**

—Mr. and Mrs. Johnnie L. Johnson are moving to Claunch. (Newspaper reading around this time revealed that many felt Claunch was a livelier and more up to date town than Gran Quivera.) [B.L.]

Mountainair Progressive, **March 24**

—There was a fire in Claunch Monday afternoon. The W. M. Pertoss wood pile burned. Probably started from coals Mr. Petross emptied in the morning.

Mountainair Progressive, **April 14**

—Gran Quivira had some important visitors Friday. Mr. Lee Trent, mayor-elect of Mountainair; Mr. Earl Parker, Mayor of Estancia; Mr. Bascom Weaver of Mountainair; and Mr. Healy of Santa Fe.

Mountainair Progressive, **May 5**

—"Mr. Mack Wells don't believe the wind will stop blowing, so moved his home into the trees so the sand won't bury it."

Mountainair Progressive, **October 20**

—Mr. and Mrs. Dean Miller attended the Shrine Convention Friday in Albuquerque.

1944 *Mountainair Progressive,* **October 27**

—Gran Quivira Wave and sailor were wed at Norfolk Naval Base. Ceremony at 5:30 P.M., October 17. Officers and enlisted personnel attend. A reception afterward. The bride's parents are Mr. and Mrs. J. M. Johnson and the groom's parents are Mr. and Mrs. Dean Miller, all of Gran Quivira.

Mountainair Progressive, **November 24**

—Mr. and Mrs. Jack Kite went to Denver to bring their

daughter home after three months in the hospital there.[14]

December 1

—Gran Quivira is covered with snow.

—Rev. Plant and wife are here conducting a meeting at the Assembly of God church.

—Mr. and Mrs. Clyde Shaw and children have moved to Lubbock.

1945 *Mountainair Progressive*

—Aunt Lou Wilson been living in very poor house; now she will have warm place in cold months built by the community.

Mountainair Progressive

—Singing conventions were held in Gran Quivera in 1945. Gospel songs—violin and mandolin accompanied.

Mountainair Progressive, **April 27**

—Mrs. Dean Miller hosted a Victory Club roll call, each member answered by telling the nicest tribute they had heard paid to President Roosevelt.

Mountainair Progressive, **June 1**

—Centerpoint five miles from Gran Quivira. A good soaking would be much appreciated out this way as many are hauling their drinking water.

—Several people from Claunch (10 miles from Gran Quivira) attended a singing at Gran Quivira. Very successful. Minister of Assembly of God church from Gallup led the revival.

Mountainair Progressive, **June 22**

—Jack Kite took six of his prize calves to the stock show in Albuquerque. He will be gone all week.

—Measles epidemic abroad.

1945 *Mountainair Messenger,* **December 29**

—Dr. Smith of Almagordo ("Doc," first caretaker of ruins) visited sons and families over the holidays.

Mountainair Progressive, **notes**

—Gospel songs used at the singing conventions. Menu

for Boys and Girls Club fairs was the usual baked beans and bean salad or boiled beans, beans and chili, stewed beans, or bean soup.

—Mrs. Dean Martin was *Mountainair Progressive* correspondent. She reported popularity of Franklin Roosevelt because the Victory Club meeting at Mrs. Dean Miller's answered roll call by calling out "F.D.R." Ladies of the Assembly of God held quilting parties to raise money to pay for a new home for Aunt Lou Wilson, the vagrant, homeless citizen of Gran Quivira, who delivered the town's babies and provided first aid and home nursing.

—War over, the village members turned to repairing and stabilizing "the ruins."

—We had an especially dry year. Six or eight families left at at once. Some were renters, some sharecroppers. Renters gave one-fourth of the crop to the landowner, sharecroppers gave half to the owner. They got tools, machinery, and equipment necessary to farm the land. Most of those who left went to California.

1945 *Mountainair Messenger,* **December 29**
—Gran Quivira covered with snow.

—Just as schools were built nearly every mile, so tiny towns (a store, church, gas station, three or four scattered houses, etc.) sprung up as satellites of larger populated places. [Editors]

Torrance Co. News, **February 15, 1954**
—There was a travel increase to Gran Quivira National Monument. Last year [1953] there were 344 visitors in 102 cars. This is a 200 percent increase in travel. Out of state cars numbered 34 percent of the total. 96 percent of the visitors viewed the exhibits.

Torrance Co. News, **March 5, Gran Quivira**
—Two pupils got 100 in spelling for the week. One was J. E. Frances.

—Movies were shown on spelling rules, three films on arithmetic, and one on the circulation of the blood. Pupils read in the *Scholastic* about the Louisiana Purchase.

—School nurse came. Everyone had gained weight in six weeks. The gains were listed.

Notes

1. This is the "Spanish Princess" that Dow married.
2. At this time, nearly every deep well dug gushed sulphur water—hence the settlement's name, "Stinking Springs." These wells would cause the parched earth to bloom and bear fruit for only three or four years (1920). They were called "Artesian wells."
3. Willard was an important town at the northern border of the Salinas Valley, which included the valley to the east of the Monzano Mountains, the locale of Gordon McMath's story. The southern end of this valley encompassed Gran Quivira and explains its involvement with a Willard newspaper. Please consult map 1.
4. Men from this area traveled to Flagstaff, Arizona, to work in the silver mines during the winter when there were no crops or other opportunities to earn money.
5. Liberty was a busy settlement near Gran Quivira, i.e., something more than just the usual schoolhouse.
6. Ardent singing was the hallmark of the fast-growing Assembly of God in the southwest at this time. "Singing Societies" were deeply religious gatherings, usually on Sunday, sometimes extended as "protracted meetings" for a week or more. White people—not indigenous, not Mexicans—took part. They were firm dispensers of pentacostalism, which they expounded with, at moments in their churches, loud singing and orgasmic enthusiasm. Our request to attend their services never took place. Sentences like "The time was changed," when we arrived at the usual hour of 7 P.M., "We will not be meeting this week," or "The minister did not arrive," represent the frustration of efforts to sing with them. We hope it was not personal, a "fear of strangers."
7. The author heard reports that an influential local family almost boasted of having an expensive Spanish sword from the loot and that it was in a barn in Carrizozo held by "two old men." (EPL, 1990.)
8. The authors found fine sand between pages of 1930–40 newspapers in the University Library.
9. Our interviews with the local people pointed out frequently the good schools in Gran Quivira and the outstandingly dedicated teachers. Names frequently mentioned were: Annie Mell (Connell), Inez Austin, Helen

Garrison, Mrs. Bowen (superintendent's wife), Bill Hamill, Mattie Hammil, Beulah Claunch, Mrs. Frank Means, Mrs. Evans, Gertrude Cobb, Annie Laurie Jackson, Pat Shaw (principal 1935–1938).

10. See again chapter 3, pp 000.
11. Mountainair and Gran Quivira could not have existed without Pop Shaffer. He was born in Harmony, Indiana, July 20, 1880, the thirteenth child of his blacksmith father and his mother. He came to Mountainair, New Mexico, in the early 1900s and started as a blacksmith—became a merchant, horse trader, land speculator, and a folk artist. His blacksmith shop burned in 1922 and he built a hardware store and implement house on the ruins; he added a second story to make a hotel. In 1931 he built an unusual stone fence and in 1932 a dining room where the hardware store had been built with its unusually decorated tables, chairs, walls, and ceiling. This work on the fence and dining room and first floor of the hotel motivated him to make small animals out of bent branches of plants and trees, bark and stones. One of these rare creatures was presented to Eleanor Roosevelt as she toured Highway 60 on her exploratory journeys of our country. Mrs. Roosevelt was enchanted by his "rare" animals. He presented her with one and every year until her death she sent him a birthday card! His home, near Mountainair, is the repository of his animals—the largest examples of folk art in New Mexico.
12. During our interview with Mr. Connell, he told of an exciting rattlesnake experience he'd had. The creature crawled up on his chest and arm as he was enjoying a nap under a tree. After some very quiet meditation he decided to fling the snake with his arm. It worked. It's sad that the abnormal fear of these useful and beautiful creatures resulting in "snake hunts" and wholesale killing is leading to their extinction. This testimony is from the author who at twelve years of age lived and played among the drylands creatures believed to be deadly, including tarantulas, black widow spiders, large (3/4-inch-long) ants, and the oldest (it is thought), the vinagaroon. They greatly need the respect of all living things.
13. The appointment of two women (Mrs. Dean Miller was the wife of the famous owner of Miller's store) a mere twenty years after women's suffrage in 1920 might be evidence that even in a small village women were encouraged in political activity to counterbalance political activism by minority men. It has been suggested that women finally were "given" suffrage for this reason.
14. The Kites had four children. One of the daughters had a health problem and remains "handicapped" to the present day. (1996) Reports always indicated she had excellent medical consultation at both Denver and Albuquerque.

Our Last Words

In pursuing the meaning or definition of a city, one finds both "numbers" and "importance" are key concepts. When we originally planned the organization of this book, we thought of writing about "The Rise and Fall of Three Villages." As we proceeded, we have felt that the three "villages" were villages in the longer purview and in modern terminology. However, when we consider the historical sweep of their existence, each of these entities could be considered "cities." They consisted of more than "average" numbers of people and they were sociologically important because they were business and cultural centers in their time.

When we began, our experience of living on this planet was in a small city in upper New York State and we had personal experiences in traveling to the major cities of the world, living in foreign countries, and undertaking graduate studies in Chicago and New York City. Naturally, we felt the pit village, the Spanish town, and the turn-of-the-century Gran Quivira were "villages." The discovery that these communities had comparatively large populations and cultural traditions and were important centers for specific reasons shifted our thinking. In our eighty years of age we became aware that in each "era" it would be unfair and almost inhumane to think any of these peoples in terms of being serfs, slaves, poor peasants, or uneducated, simple people. Each stage of growth of the three communities will impress one with the humanity, passion, and capacity to work, play, sing, and enjoy beauty of the people who lived in this area and era.

Each period grew out of the one preceding it. The "future" of each grew from interactions with the past. We feel more than ever the power of history on human behavior. The more human beings observe, study and reflect on "place" and "time," the better they can understand themselves and all the variant "others" with whom they interact. Views bear little wisdom without vistas.

Mr. and Mrs. McMath with the folk art created by Mr. McMath and recognized by the *Smithsonian Magazine*.

Appendixes

Appendix A
Interview with Jack and Louise Kite, January 21, 1996

We were greeted warmly. Mr. Kite is tall, erect, and a little deaf. He related he was born in Okra, Texas, in 1908. He came to Gran Quivira when he was twenty-two years old. He had heard from a young male relative that he could get a job putting in fence posts for two dollars a day and room and board. In Texas he was working for a stockman who paid him $35 a month with room and board. He did not like the man for whom he was working in Texas. He worked for his employer's brother and was treated kindly, and allowed to eat and live with the family. However, his employer was different. He was not kind. Jack was anxious for a change.

The fence post job was placing a fence around the Forest Preserve and was in the charge of a Texas contractor. "We lived in a camp. The boss's name was Roach. He was a decent fellow."

Mrs. Kite, his wife—a friendly, warm, outgoing personality, poised and eager to be helpful—was also born in Texas. She came to New Mexico as a baby in a covered wagon drawn by horses and mules, with an extended family, in hopes her father's health would improve in this new location. Her father's biography appears in the Torrance County edition of *New Mexico History*.

Our discussion began with the concept of a Gran Quivira community. "Yes—there was a Gran Quivira community—a marked one earlier in this century, but now it hardly exists." In those days it was called Grand Quivera (spelled with a "e"). It extended from Mountainair to Claunch and from the Vernie Wells home to the Lewis home—a little beyond the White Oaks Cemetery where it crosses into Soccoro. In the early days, many people lived in the community. Mrs. Kite made a list (see appendix) of people she could recall who lived in the community.

There were stores owned by "Diamond Tooth" Miller (he had a diamond filling in one of his teeth) and Grandfather Wilson's store. There was a barber shop and Mrs. Kite's father started a large store and Conoco station in 1924. The main road ran through Grand Quivira and was the Main Street. The community church, "The Assembly of God," was the center of much social activity. There were "Literaries"—reading of poetry and plays, sometimes serious and sometimes "funny."

There was a quilt- and mattress-manufacturing establishment. Women went there to help make quilts and mattresses. They made quilts and added handiwork.

One of Mrs. Kite's most vivid memories was when her father homesteaded in Grand Quivira in the good crop year of 1921. The grass (harvested to feed animals in winter) was one foot high—even higher. The crops were abundant: watermelons, cantaloupe, potatoes, pinto beans, corn, pumpkins, and squash. Her father took the produce to Mountainair with a wagon and burros. They camped all night at Comforts and then proceeded to Mountainair. At the time there were two elevators in Mountainair. The beans were cleaned and sacked and sent all over the country.

A considerable amount of the interview was involved with the subject of WATER. The bean crop industry was especially dependent on water. Upon inquiry on the reality of Spanish priests growing apple trees, pear, plum, and apricot trees at the ruins, Mr. Kite said, "It depends on when the rains came. If they came at the right time, generous crops will result. We have had apple trees in our backyard for ten years—one year we had apples." Mr. and Mrs. Kite live on the property Mrs. Kite's family bought and have owned since homesteading in 1918. Their comfortable home was built in 1970. Mr. Kite is very familiar with "the water problem."

"In the 1930s we had an especially dry year. Six or eight families left all at once. Some were renters and some were sharecroppers. Renters gave one fourth of the crop to the owner of the land. The sharecropper gave one half of the crop to the owner. In this latter case the owner supplied the tools, machinery and equipment necessary to farm the land. A number of the families later went to California," reported Mr. Kite.

According to the Kites, the school, post office, and church played vital roles in the Gran Quivira community. "The children really liked school. Some had horses and they would pick up 'walkers' and the new passengers would ride behind the saddle." Most schools had only elementary grades but one had three years of high school. The teachers were excellent and well liked. Mrs. Bright, the wife of Superintendent Bright, was recalled as a local teacher.

The post office was moved nearer the other stores in 1931 or 1932. Mack Wells was the last postmaster. He was assisted by Retha Collins. Mack broke his arm and went to the hospital and died. Then the post office closed.

"At one time 150 people regularly attended the church [Assembly of God]. We had lots of children in Sunday school. Now we have three to five [January 1990]. There is a young clergyman who comes every Sunday and we have services in the morning and at 7 o'clock in the evening. We support the church by tithing." They continued by explaining that those who remained in the church had survived during the droughts, the emigration during the hard times, but that their own four children had all moved away. "The church remains a vital institution—perhaps now the chief institution of the community."

Jack stated the Park Service began digging the ruins in 1923. "This," he said, "was contrary to information that universities were responsible for the first digging." Mr. Toulaine was the superintendent after Doc Smith.

Mr. Kite worked at first two days a week on the day Mr. Pinkley had off. Mr. Pinkley came from the southwestern region (Blackwater, Arizona) and he lived in the house "Doc" Smith had built to live in. (It is still standing in January 1991.) Mr. Kite worked part-time until he became a 180-day permanent part-time worker. He recalls an amusing experience: One hot day some visitors got out of the car and inquired of Mr. Kite, "Why did you put those ruins so far from town?"

When the park attendants were moving from one building to another they were putting the visitor registers on the junk heap. Jack asked whether he could have them. Every page is an interesting record of the early days. People came by horse, by car, and on foot. The car most commonly named was Ford. The reactions of the visitors recorded are delightful. The earliest is 1923. These books are among the favorite treasures of the Kites, who have gathered rocks, stones, shards, and all kinds of artifacts on their property.

Mrs. Kite recalled that in about 1932 the museum at that time was "robbed." Everything was stolen. "In a way, not much that was really valuable was taken." Articles were chiefly a Spanish dagger, pots, skeletal bones, and shards that had been found.

"The building which now is the Visitors' Center was formerly the superintendent's home. It was built in 1934 by government contract."

One could not meet more devoted people to the ruins, to Grand Quivira and to the National Park.*

*Jack Kite:
  Born in Okra, Texas, May 19, 1908
  Moved to Gran Quivira in 1930
  Married Louise Turner 1931
  Farmed 1931–1945
  Cattleman and registered horseman 1940 to present time (1996)
  Gran Quivira employee 1945–1977

Appendix B
Residents of Gran Quivira

Residents who lived in Gran Quivira as reported by Louise Kite to Beulah Link, February 1, 1991.

Mr. and Mrs Carl Evans
John and Stella Smith and family
Mr. and Mrs. Glen Vines—on ranch little farther north than Wayne Connell's
Mr. and Mrs. Homer Jackson—on ranch with a big well (not drinking water)
Wayne and Melody Connell and family
Rev. John St. John and family—Galloway House—minister of Assembly of God church
Mr. and Mrs. John Johnson—Louise Turner's uncle—lived by a well
Opal and Nancy Johnson—by present corral
Truman and Pauline Thornton—Louise Kite's sister—lived in Turner's Store
John and Lexie Adams and family
Mr. and Mrs. Ladd and family—J. J. Robinson's daughter
Mrs. Slac
Cousin Fred and Fay Russell and family—distant relatives of Louise Kite's mother
T. E. Eldridge and family—lived in the Lacky house
Elbert Smith and family—lived in Kerr house

Halley and Voda Yaughboro and family—lived in Allison House—cousin to the Allisons— in the Thomas house

Jack and Louise Kite

Stennie Russell and family

Widow Jones and family—lived in Thomas house

Slim and Hattie Kite and family—Jack Kite's nephew lived in Wiswold house

Clyde and Wanda Jackson

Mrs. Carl Evans and children

Hershell, Opal Fulfer, and family—lived in Kerr house

Rev. Br. Chaney and Sr. Chaney and family

Mr. Stewart—owned house next to Smith's

C. N. and Allene Fulfer—had store in Miller's Store and lived there also

Felton and Louise Fulfer and boys—lived in Turner's Store

Slim and Rose Bud Bishop—lived in Kerr house

Mr. and Mrs. Weir—had store in Miller's Store and lived there

Mack Wells and his wife, Margie—lived in Miller's Store and had the post office—Mack died and then Reatha Connell had the post office—we lost the post office then

Gus and Matlin McBride

Rev. and Sister Harris

Travis Maples and wife

"Lots of people lived in the Monument Ruins from time to time."—Louise Kite Feb. 1, 1991

Appendix C
Teachers in Gran Quivira Schools as Recalled by Louise Kite

Pat Shaw, principal
Annie Mell Austin
Inez Austin
Helen Garrison
Mrs. Bowen (superintendent's wife)
Bill Hammill
Mattie Hammill (Bill's sister)
Beulah Claunch
Mrs. Frank Means (Bessie)
Mrs. Evans
Gertrude Cobb

Postmasters and Postmistresses

The Dows (Ida)
J. J. Robinson
Irvin Smith and Doc Smith
Mr. and Mrs. Frank Means
Mrs. Beatty
Mrs. Beatty Igzor

Mrs. "Doc" Miller
Weir family
Mack Wells
Reatha Connell—finished up—our post office was closed

Appendix D
Selected Readings

1. Bennett, Richard H. *An Archeological Survey of Gran Guivera*, 1981.
2. Carleton, Maj. James Henry. Diary.
3. Crawford, Stanley, *Major Domo*.
4. Fite, Gilbert C. *The Farmer's Frontier, 1865–1900*.
5. Hays, Alden, Jon Young and A. H. Warren, *Excavation of Mound Seven*. National Park Service, 1981.
6. Hickerson, Nancy. *Humanas*.
7. Keleher, William A. *Violence in Lincoln County, 1869–1881*.
8. Liston, Florence C. And Robert H. *Those Who Come Before*.
9. Looney, Ralph. *The Ghost Towns of New Mexico*. New York: Hastings House Publishers.
10. Rautman, Allison E. *The 1994 Field Season at LA—199 Kite Pueblo, Torrence County, New Mexico*.
11. Sauer, Carl. *Land and Live*. 1963.
12. Tainter, Joseph A. *Cultural Resources Overview*. Forest Service, Albuquerque, New Mexico.
13. Thwaites, Reuben. *Commerce of the Prairies, 1831–39*.
14. Underhill, Ruth M. *First Penthouse Dwellers of America*. New York: J. J. Augustin.
15. Wallace, Susan. *Land of Pueblos*.
16. Walter, Paul. *Cities That Died of Fear*.
17. Waters, Frank. *People of the Valley*.
18. Willison, Robert. *Gran Quivira*.
19. Westways 1960. *A Thousand Years at Grand Quivira*.

SWEET SMELLING MYRRH.

THE

AUTOBIOGRAPHY OF MADAME GUYON.

EDITED BY

ABBIE C. MORROW,

Author of Bible Morning Glories, Bible B's, Etc.

ISBN 0-88019-348-4

Schmul Publishing Co., Inc.
Wesleyan Book Club   1996   Salem, Ohio

Printed by
Old Paths Tract Society, Inc.
Route 2, Box 43
Shoals, Indiana 47581